THE BOOK OF
ROLEX

JENS HØY & CHRISTIAN FROST

THE BOOK OF
ROLEX

ACC ART BOOKS

CONTENTS

Foreword 7

The Rolex Story 11

Cosmograph Daytona 21

The World's Most Expensive Rolex 33

Explorer 37

A Rolex is 100 Per Cent Swiss-Made 45

The Classic Oyster 47

When Your Rolex Needs Servicing 55

The Classic Rolex Datejust 63

The Pilot's Watch: Air-King 71

Materials 77

The Bracelet 79

The Movement 81

A Rolex Needs Time 83

The Presidents' Watch: Day-Date 87

When a Rolex Becomes Vintage 95

Vintage from Rolex 99

The Hunt for a Red Sub 101

THE BOOK OF ROLEX

The Pilot's Watch: GMT-Master **103**

The Businessman's Watch: Sky-Dweller **109**

The Fake Rolex **114**

Frankenstein **119**

How to Spot a Fake Rolex **122**

The Science Watch: Milgauss **125**

The Workhorse: Submariner **131**

Know Your Rolex's Nickname **138**

Day-Date Puzzle-Motif **147**

The Captain's Watch: Yacht-Master **153**

For the Lady in Your Life: Lady Datejust **163**

Submariner Ultra: Sea-Dweller **171**

The King of Diving Watches: Deepsea **177**

Rolex's Dress Watch: Perpetual 1908 **183**

Rolex's Secret Model: Cellini **189**

The Doctor's Watch **193**

Rolex's Forgotten Brother: Tudor **197**

The Selfless Benefactor **205**

THE BOOK OF
ROLEX

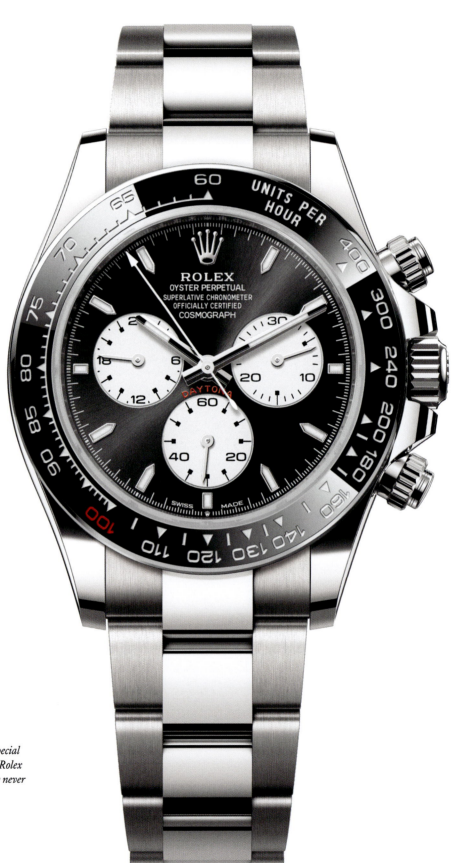

The **COSMOGRAPH DAYTONA** *in the special* **LE MANS EDITION** *is the watch that all Rolex enthusiasts dream of, but will probably never own. You can read why on* **PAGE 33**.

THE BOOK OF
ROLEX

FOREWORD

When we decided to write a book about Rolex back in 2014, we had no idea that it would end up becoming the internationally bestselling book ever about Rolex. This is the third edition; the English edition was first published in 2019 and, so far, it has seen nine print runs.

The fascination with Rolex can be hard to explain. For most people, the day they buy their first Rolex is the culmination of an interest that began many years before and often marks a special event in their lives. This applies to those who buy a new Rolex as well as those who delve into the many vintage models. The fascination is usually to do with the mechanics and the history behind the watch, as every Rolex model has its own unique story. In the modern world, there is something reassuring about a mechanical watch, hand assembled in Switzerland and developed at its own majestic pace over more than a century.

Of course, one often encounters people's prejudices, usually in the form of outrage over spending so much money on a watch, completely unaware of how solid an investment a Rolex is. A Rolex is something you value and take care of, so it lasts long enough to be passed down to your son or daughter, who will think of you every time they look at it.

Perhaps that's what a Rolex is all about, for what other product can truly do that today?

> A Rolex is something you value and take care of, so it lasts long enough to be passed down to your son or daughter, who will think of you every time they look at it

THE BOOK OF
ROLEX

THE MOVEMENT *is the very heart of a Rolex, in this case the* **CALIBRE 4132** *from the special Le Mans anniversary model of the* **DAYTONA**. *Perhaps that's why this particular model was given a transparent caseback, so it's not just your* **WATCHMAKER** *who can* **ADMIRE IT.**

ROLEX OYSTER FROM 1953, *which is* WATERPROOF *to a depth of* **100 METRES**. *It was this model that evolved into* ROLEX'S *successful* SUBMARINER SERIES.

THE BOOK OF
ROLEX

THE ROLEX
STORY

The story of Rolex is the story of an orphaned boy, born in Germany, who created the world's most iconic watch, which helped plan the Great Escape during WWII

Rolex watches are seen on the wrists of artists and businessmen, doctors and mechanics, as well as presidents and hip-hop stars with millions in the bank. They come in a range of prices, from the fairly inexpensive Air-King to the Daytona in platinum, which costs more than most of us spend on a car. A Rolex can be steel or precious metal, decorated with diamonds and gems in all the colours of the rainbow, and on top of that, there are the vintage models, which, in terms of value, span the entire price range.

It's fair to claim then, that Rolex might have the most diverse range of customers anywhere. The brand itself is an icon and, love it or loathe it, you will have an opinion about it. For some, Rolex's classic design and rich tradition are the definition of the classic Swiss watch. For others, Rolex is nothing more than a rather gaudy way to demonstrate wealth and success, as was indeed the case with the yuppie generation in the 1980s. However, the story of Rolex is so much more than that.

It started in 1905, when Hans Wilsdorf and Alfred Davis, who were related by marriage, decided to become business partners. Wilsdorf & Davis imported watch movements from Aegler in Switzerland, and set them in watches made by British watchmakers. The watches were then sold to London jewellers, who stamped their own name on the dial; the only trace of Wilsdorf & Davis was the initials 'W&D' on the back of the watchcase.

Then, in 1908, Hans Wilsdorf registered the name 'Rolex'. Though still living in London at the time, he opened an office in La Chaux-

de-Fonds in Switzerland. How Wilsdorf came up with the name 'Rolex' has been discussed at length among watch aficionados. The official explanation from Wilsdorf himself was that he wanted a name short enough to fit on the dial of a watch, that could be pronounced in any language. A more romantic explanation is that Wilsdorf was inspired by the distinct sound of winding a Swiss watch movement.

The quality of the watches from Wilsdorf & Davis quickly made a name for themselves, and in 1914 they were awarded a Class A precision certificate by the renowned Kew Observatory. This certification was normally only bestowed upon watches used by the Royal Navy, since successful navigation of the seven seas depended upon being able to tell the time with great accuracy. This same year, 1914, also marked the start of WWI, which spelled the end for Wilsdorf & Davis and the advent of Rolex.

The outbreak of war meant higher taxes on luxury goods like gold, silver and Swiss watch movements, and so the watches from Wilsdorf & Davis simply became too expensive. In 1919, Wilsdorf & Davis left London for Geneva, and changed the name to the Rolex Watch Company. In the years to come, the name would be changed to Montres Rolex SA and then to Rolex SA. Wilsdorf never forgot about London and England, which he demonstrated when the world went to war once again.

British soldiers would often purchase a Rolex, since it had greater accuracy and was more robust than the standard issue Army watch. And so it was that a Rolex watch came to play a decisive part in what came to be known as the Great Escape.

> Rolex watches are seen on the wrists of artists and businessmen, doctors and mechanics, presidents and hip-hop stars with millions in the bank

THE BOOK OF
ROLEX

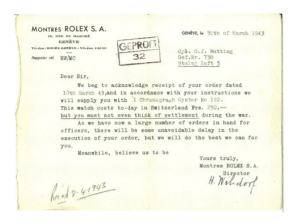 

ROLEX *sent some 3,000 watches to British officers held captive in* **GERMAN POW CAMPS** *during WWII. This letter, signed by* **HANS WILSDORF** *himself, was sent to* **C.J. NUTTING**, *who used his* **ROLEX OYSTER CHRONOGRAPH** *to time the German guards, as he planned* **THE GREAT ESCAPE**.

Hans Wilsdorf had a reputation for being generous, which he demonstrated during WWII. When British soldiers were captured, the German soldiers would often take their Rolex watches. When Wilsdorf heard of this, he made it possible for British officers to order new watches from Rolex. These watches were delivered to the German POW camps from Switzerland with the help of the Red Cross. The watch would be accompanied by a letter, often signed by Wilsdorf himself, instructing the recipient not to make any attempt to pay for the watch until after the war. All in all, some 3,000 Rolex watches were delivered to British officers this way.

Wilsdorf was born in Germany but lived most of his life in London, so it might also have been a way to demonstrate that his sympathies were with the allied forces. The arrangement was restricted to British officers, with notable exceptions such as corporal Clive James Nutting. Before being enlisted Nutting worked as a shoemaker, which was quite useful in a POW camp like Stalag Luft III. The British officers in the camp had given him their recommendations, so Nutting wrote a letter to Rolex requesting a watch.

That watch was delivered to Stalag Luft III on 10 July 1943. What Hans Wilsdorf didn't know was that Nutting was part of what was later to be known as the Great Escape, when 250 British officers intended to escape. This would result in an embarrassing humiliation for the Germans, who were convinced that escaping from a camp like Stalag Luft III was impossible. The German high command would also need to direct important resources away from the front as they attempted to recapture the escaped prisoners before they made their way back to England.

Normally, the captured British officers would order the Rolex Speedking, the forerunner to the Air-King and Rolex entry-level model. However, Nutting ordered the much more expensive Rolex Oyster 3525 Chronograph, since he needed the chronograph function to time the German patrols in the camp, in order to calculate how many prisoners could escape at a time.

After months of careful planning, Nutting put his plan into action on the night of 25 March 1944. All in all, 76 Allied airmen escaped Stalag Luft III before the Germans sounded the alarm. However, only three made it out of Germany. The rest were either captured or shot. C.J. Nutting survived but spent the rest of the war being transferred between different prison camps. He managed to keep his Rolex, though. In 1945, Nutting had returned to Britain and wrote a letter to Hans Wilsdorf, revealing how his Rolex was used to plan the Great Escape. He also asked Wilsdorf to send the final invoice. It didn't arrive until 1948 and, due to currency restrictions, Rolex could only make it out for £15 ($19) — a small amount for an Oyster 3525 Chronograph, even then.

However, the story of the Great Escape made it around the world, and did much for Rolex's fortunes, especially in America, when it became a movie starring Steve McQueen.

Nutting kept his watch until he passed away at his home in Australia in 2001, aged 90. A few years later his famous watch was sold at auction for an impressive £66,000 ($86,000).

> The Rolex ordered by C.J. Nutting arrived at Stalag Luft III on 10 July 1943. What Hans Wilsdorf didn't know was that it was needed to plan the Great Escape

HANS WILSDORF (1881–1960), *born in* **GERMANY,** *was orphaned as a child. He trained as a watchmaker, working for a Swiss watch manufacturer in* **LA CHAUX-DE-FONDS,** *but moved to* **LONDON** *where he founded what later became* **ROLEX SA.**

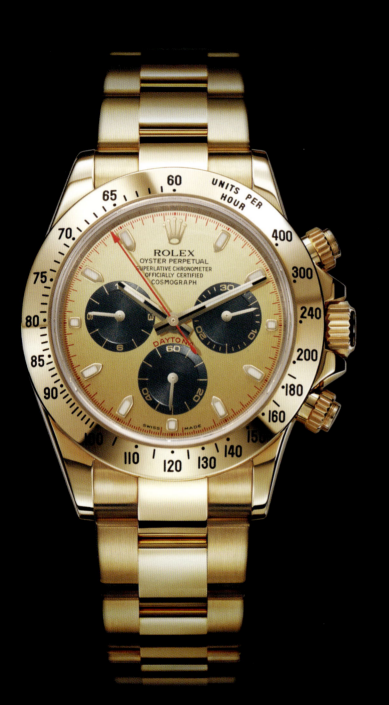

Above, the first **ROLEX OYSTER** *from 1926, the world's first* **WATERPROOF WRISTWATCH**, *and to the left, the legendary* **COSMOGRAPH DAYTONA** *in gold. Below, the first* **MOVEMENT** *from Rolex, which made the whole thing* **POSSIBLE**.

THE BOOK OF
ROLEX

Very few pictures exist from **STALAG LUFT III**, *the WWII POW camp. The mastermind behind the Great Escape,* **C.J. NUTTING**, *is seen on the left in the picture.* **THE GREAT ESCAPE** *became a movie with* **STEVE MCQUEEN**, *but without* **ROLEX** *it would never have happened.*

In 1944, a year before WWII ended, Hans Wilsdorf's wife passed away. Needless to say, this left Wilsdorf deeply saddened, but it also made him very aware of his own mortality and worried about what would become of the company he had created. He had spent the majority of his life as an orphan, since both his parents passed away before he was 12 years old. By this time Rolex SA was already a giant in the watch industry, and its products were in great demand, especially in America. The story of how Rolex had sent watches to British officers in German POW camps had made a great impression.

More than anything, though, Wilsdorf was worried that Rolex SA would become a public company in the event of his passing. The result of this would be that the money Rolex made would end up in the pockets of already wealthy investors. This was the last thing Wilsdorf wanted to happen and, as a result, he decided to bequeath his shares to a trust, in order to ensure that Rolex would never become a public company, and that part of the profits from Rolex would go to charity.

This is the reason you can't buy shares in Rolex SA on any stock exchange. It also means that Rolex is shrouded in mystery. In fact, it's more or less impossible to get any information on Rolex, other than what Rolex choose to reveal. In fact, we don't even know for sure how many watches Rolex produces every year. A qualified guess would be 2,000 watches a day, which means an annual profit of nearly £6 billion ($8 billion). This would make Rolex irresistible to the Gordon Gekkos of this world, if it were a public company. But thanks to Wilsdorf, it never will be.

However, Rolex didn't become a success by accident. The reason Wilsdorf went into business in the first place was to make high-quality watches for a reasonable price. A Rolex might seem very expensive, but in fact it's more or less impossible to find another hand-assembled Swiss wristwatch that is more affordable.

Wilsdorf never stopped pushing the limits of what was possible. The first Oyster model from 1926 was also the world's first waterproof wristwatch, and the first Submariner from 1953 was the first divers' watch able to remain waterproof at depths of 100 metres. Today, the diving watches from Rolex are legendary. This legend was forged when the Rolex Deepsea went to the bottom of the Mariana Trench, attached to the bathyscaphe *Trieste* with French explorer Jacques Piccard. From inside the *Trieste*, Piccard could observe the watch ticking away, despite the enormous pressure at the deepest point in the ocean, and later wrote a telegram to Wilsdorf: 'I am delighted to inform you, that your watch is as accurate at the depth of 11,000 metres as it is on the surface.'

Since then Rolex has created watches that are both timeless and innovative. If imitation is the most sincere form of flattery, then Rolex has been the subject of much flattery indeed. A Rolex is a mechanical masterpiece that will last more than a lifetime, and is frequently passed on from parent to child. There are those who will never see a Rolex as anything more than a distasteful display of wealth, as demonstrated by the yuppie generation of the 1980s. However, this really couldn't be further from the truth, or from the life of Hans Wilsdorf, the 19th-century orphaned German boy.

> Today, Rolex is owned by a foundation, as Hans Wilsdorf was concerned that the money from his life's work would end up in the pockets of already wealthy speculators

17

Your Rolex is **HAND-ASSEMBLED,** *and everything is manufactured at Rolex's factories in Switzerland. Only Rolex know exactly* **HOW MANY WATCHES** *they produce each year and how long each watch takes to make, but most estimate that it takes about* **A YEAR TO CREATE A ROLEX** *from start to finish.*

Rolex don't do **RETRO**! *And yet, the latest generation of the legendary* **COSMOGRAPH DAYTONA** *has clearly drawn its inspiration from* **THE CLASSIC MODELS.**

THE BOOK OF
ROLEX

COSMOGRAPH
DAYTONA

For many watch aficionados, the Daytona is above and beyond any other model
from Rolex and, to this day, it remains the world's most sought-after chronograph

The legendary **PAUL NEWMAN DIAL**, *here fitted with the black dial. An entire book could be written about the details of this particular model.*

You had to **WIND** *the early Daytona by hand! It didn't become an* **AUTOMATIC** *until 1988, and then only with a movement produced by* **ZENITH**.

The Daytona was originally called the **LE MANS**. *But when Rolex became the official sponsor of the race on* **DAYTONA SPEEDWAY**, *the name was changed. Winners of the race still receive an engraved* **ROLEX DAYTONA**.

DAYTONA *was the first Rolex with subdials in a contrasting colour. The unique* **ART DECO STYLE** *on this model wasn't very popular in its day.*

The **WATCH BEZEL** *is designed to measure speed. If you were at Le Mans in 1964 and watched Jackie Stewart pass by in his* **FERRARI 250 GTO**, *you could determine how fast he was going.*

There was a time when you could walk into any Rolex dealer's and leave with a mechanical **PAUL NEWMAN DIAL** *for a three-figure sum. These days it will be six figures.*

THE BOOK OF
ROLEX

The ROLEX DAYTONA in platinum is recognised by its distinctive ICE-BLUE DIAL COLOUR. Platinum is used both for the watchcase and in the bracelet.

EVEROSE GOLD is Rolex's answer to ROSE GOLD, which is gold alloyed with PLATINUM to prevent the material from losing its distinctive pinkish hue.

The ROLEX DAYTONA IN WHITE GOLD is now also available with the special rubber strap called OYSTERFLEX, which was introduced with the YACHT-MASTER and is constructed around a core of TITANIUM.

Here, WHITE GOLD is used for the WATCH-CASE, BEZEL and central links of the BRACELET. This provides a unique lustre, is exclusive and subtly REFINED.

THE BOOK OF
ROLEX

 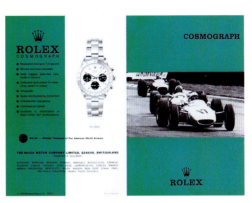 

Selling the **ROLEX DAYTONA**. *To the left, the original* **DAYTONA** *from 1963, when the model was called the* **ROLEX LE MANS**. *To the right, the Hollywood star and racing driver* **PAUL NEWMAN** *wearing a* **DAYTONA**. *This model is affectionately known as the* **PAUL NEWMAN DIAL**.

The first thing you notice is the word 'cosmograph'. Rolex have never explained what it means. 'Cosmo' could come from the Greek word 'cosmos', used by Pythagoras to describe the order of the universe, primarily involving time, space and movement. 'Graph' perhaps from the Greek 'grapho', meaning to write. So, a cosmograph is an instrument for tracking the time it takes for objects to move through time and space.

When the first Cosmograph Daytona was introduced, it distinguished itself from Rolex's earlier chronograph models. The scale, previously on the dial itself, was now engraved on the bezel for easier use, and the small subdials had contrasting colours. This scale, used with the stopwatch, calculates, for example, the speed of a racing car over 1,000 metres. If the stopwatch hand stops after 30 seconds, using the scale on the bezel you can see that the speed was 120 km/h.

In the first advertisements from 1963, Rolex referred to the model as the Le Mans. However, since 1962, Rolex had been sponsoring the 24-hour race at Daytona Beach in Florida, and in 1964, the term 'Daytona' was applied to Rolex's new Cosmograph. Initially the model wasn't successful, although it remained largely unchanged until 1987. Its main drawback was its mechanical movement, requiring daily winding. Another issue was that accidentally pressing the chronograph buttons, such as in a swimming pool, could flood the movement with water. Rolex attempted to address this with the 'screw-down crown', securing the crown and side buttons to prevent accidental activation.

> The screw-down crown made the watch more difficult to wind. In a world where quartz movements were the must-have feature, no one cared about the Rolex Daytona

However, this also made it more cumbersome to wind the watch. In a world where quartz watches were the big news, few were interested in a Daytona. They languished in Rolex dealers' showcases for years, often sold at nearly half-price when they eventually found buyers. In 1988, Rolex finally introduced the Daytona with Zenith's Calibre 400 from 1969. It was the only self-winding movement (also known as automatic) that met Rolex's high standards, despite extensive modifications. They couldn't have chosen a better time, as collecting wristwatches reached its peak in those years. Collectors vied to secure the last examples of the manual Daytona before it was discontinued, as well as the first examples of the new model, which were produced in limited quantities due to Zenith's limited supply of their Calibre 400. The result was a several-year waiting list for a Rolex Daytona.

There are three series of the Daytona. The first is known by its four-digit reference numbers, such as Ref. 6239 (the legendary 'Paul Newman Dial'). The second series, with the Zenith Calibre 400, has a five-digit reference number, starting with Ref. 16520. In 2000, Ref. 116520 was introduced with the so-called Calibre 4130, Rolex's first new movement in 50 years. The Daytona was now entirely Rolex, and it is this third series that we have today. The Daytona model has never been more popular, especially as vintage models. It's no coincidence that the world's most expensive watch is also a Rolex Daytona, specifically the watch that belonged to the actor Paul Newman...

DIAMONDS ARE FOREVER – *and so is a Rolex,* ALMOST. *Here's the model launched in 2024, featuring a* WHITE-GOLD CASE, *a bezel set with 36 diamonds, and a dial available in white or black* MOTHER-OF-PEARL.

THE BOOK OF ROLEX

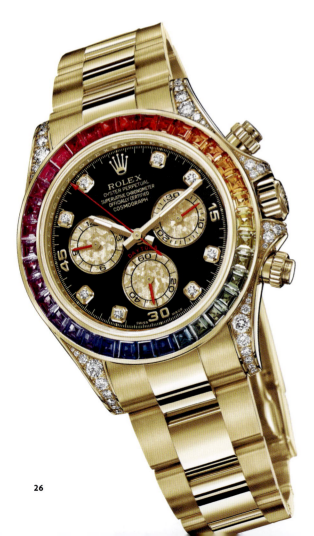

DAYTONA 'LEOPARD'
You need a little something extra to pull off a **LEOPARD** *– like* **STEVEN TYLER**, *lead singer with Aerosmith. It is by far the most extreme design from Rolex, and marked the* **50TH ANNIVERSARY** *for the Daytona in 2005. A Leopard was auctioned for* **£63,000 ($82,000)** *at Christie's, which was twice the estimate. It's produced in limited numbers because the* **36 YELLOW SAPPHIRES** *on the bezel are extremely rare. The official price is about* **£41,000 ($54,000)**, *but be prepared to wait several years to take delivery.*

DAYTONA PLATINUM WITH DIAMONDS
If platinum in itself won't quite do the job, you can add **DIAMONDS ON THE BEZEL AND DIAL**. *This model was introduced at* **BASELWORLD 2014** *with bracelet and watchcase in platinum. There are 36 diamonds on the bezel and* **437 DIAMONDS** *in the dial, with hands in* **WHITE GOLD TINTED BLUE**. *The price? Around £130,000 ($170,000).*

DAYTONA 'RAINBOW'
Every year the manufacturers get together for **BASELWORLD** *in Switzerland. In 2012, this is where Rolex launched the* **DAYTONA RAINBOW**. *Apart from diamonds and subdials in a special mix of gold and crystal, the Rainbow has a bezel with* **SAPPHIRES IN ALL THE COLOURS OF THE RAINBOW**. *The gems are selected with great care and give a unique glow, even if it might be a bit over the top for most of us!*

THE FIRST DAYTONA
1963 *was the year of the first* **ROLEX COSMOGRAPH DAYTONA**. *Originally it was called the* **LE MANS**, *but Rolex was the official sponsor for the race at* **DAYTONA SPEEDWAY**, *so the name was changed. Collectors still refer to the first edition as the 'Le Mans'. The winner of the* **ROLEX 24 HOURS AT DAYTONA** *receives an engraved Daytona, as do the winning team at the 24-hour race at* **LE MANS**.

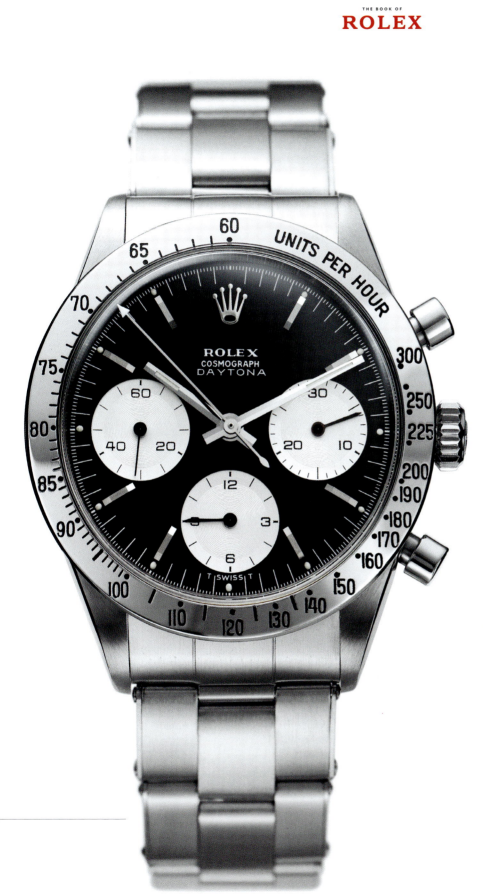

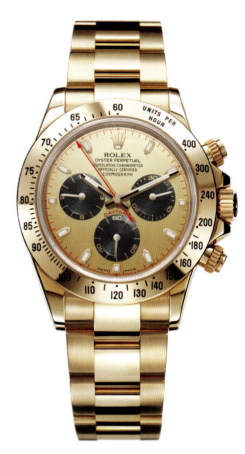

DAYTONA IN GOLD

GOLD WATCHES aren't for everyone, but they are rarely as elegant as this. The Daytona is available in **18-CARAT GOLD** and somehow Rolex gets away with it. It might have something to do with the **CLASSIC DESIGN**, which has stood the test of time, over and over again.

DAYTONA REF. 6263

It was introduced in the **1970S** and it wasn't very successful. Rolex's dealers would offer them at **HALF PRICE** and they still wouldn't sell. Today you'll pay well over **£18,000 ($23,000)** for a Ref. 6263.

THE BOOK OF ROLEX

THE BACK *of the Le Mans edition of the* **DAYTONA** *features a glass case, allowing the fortunate owner to admire the special movement called* **CALIBRE 4132**, *found exclusively here. It's possibly only Rolex that would create a truly special* **ANNIVERSARY MODEL**, *highly sought after by everyone, produce only a few examples, and then* **DISCONTINUE IT**.

It is extremely unusual for Rolex to introduce an anniversary model, but at the annual watch fair in Geneva in 2023, Rolex did just that, creating the most coveted wristwatch of the year!

To celebrate the 100th anniversary of Le Mans, Rolex launched a very special edition of the Daytona with a new bezel, a modified dial, and an original newly developed movement. The new Daytona 'Le Mans' was truly something special in every way, although initially it was difficult to categorise. It wasn't a re-edition of a classic model, nor was it a homage, as Rolex doesn't typically engage in such practices – and yet, the inspiration from the legendary Paul Newman Dial is evident, along with the aesthetics of the early Daytona models, which themselves have a clear connection to Le Mans.

There's a quirky twist in the story, though. When Rolex were gearing up to launch their brand-new chronograph in 1963, it wasn't called Daytona – instead, it was referred to as the 'Le Mans' in the initial advertisements. What happened in the meantime was that Rolex became the sponsor of the Daytona 24-hour race, prompting the renaming of the new model. The new Daytona 'Le Mans' is actually a fusion of the original Daytona and elements from the iconic Paul Newman Dial, all united in a completely fresh interpretation. At first glance, it may appear to be a regular Daytona, but the more you study it, the more differences you discover in the details.

First and foremost, there's the red marking on the bezel, a subtle detail that once seen, is hard to live without. Then there's the slimmer typography on the bezel itself, a nod back to the early Daytona models, and the three subdials, a romantic interpretation reminiscent of the Paul Newman Dial model.

It's all rounded off to perfection by using white gold – unmistakably exclusive yet appropriately understated for those who don't recognise it. If you wear a Daytona in the Le Mans edition and encounter a Rolex enthusiast along your way, be prepared to be late for your next meeting!

Another detail of the Le Mans model is the movement itself. The latest generation of Daytona models comes with the brand-new Calibre 4131 movement. However, the chronograph function can only be used for 12 hours at a time, which isn't suitable for a 24-hour race. Therefore, the Le Mans edition of the Daytona is equipped with Calibre 4132, allowing for the chronograph function to be used for 24 hours.

Only a few examples of the Le Mans edition were made, far fewer than Rolex could have sold. In early 2024, something even more shocking happened than the initial launch of the model – Rolex discontinued it. This means the few examples that were produced are now worth their weight in gold. The Rolex model with reference number 126529LN is no longer available but will forever remain highly sought after...

> The Daytona was originally called the Le Mans. But when Rolex became the official sponsor of the Daytona 24-hour race the name was changed

THE WORLD'S MOST EXPENSIVE WRISTWATCH *is the* **ROLEX DAYTONA** *that once belonged to* **PAUL NEWMAN**, *and which was sold at auction in New York in 2017 for* **$17,752,500** *(nearly £14 million). The watch was a gift from Newman's partner,* **JOANNE WOODWARD**, *when he began racing cars at a later age, explaining the inscription:* '**DRIVE CAREFULLY ME**'.

Photo: Copyright Philips Auctioneers LLC

NEWMAN'S OWN®
ORGANICS

my father was having a
s restoring for the fam
tuck R
e of th
nt th

e good
e Nell Ne
g ideas, an
ecided to
nds. I sup

r is to ackno
l Rolex Dayto
Woodward. I wis
r, to my father. Jam
dship with my father an
stions about the authenti
ce in California. I can be re

Sincerely,
Nell Newman

ROLEX COSMOGRAPH DAYTONA

UNITS PER HOUR

WATCH COLLECTORS *around the world had been searching for* PAUL NEWMAN'S ROLEX DAYTONA *without success until it suddenly surfaced in* NEW YORK. *No one knows who bought it, so is this the* LAST TIME *we'll see it?*

2098, Ap

THE BOOK OF
ROLEX

THE WORLD'S MOST EXPENSIVE ROLEX

Paul Newman's own watch, given to him by his wife, actor Joanne Woodward, was considered the holy grail among watch collectors for decades. The problem was that no one knew its whereabouts or who owned it, despite collectors worldwide searching tirelessly for it. That is, until it suddenly appeared at Phillips' auction house in New York in 2017, along with the story of its journey. In 1984, Paul Newman had gifted it to his daughter's then boyfriend, James Cox, who had owned it ever since. Back in 1984, when James Cox received Paul Newman's watch, a similar one could be bought for around $200 (£167). It wouldn't be an understatement to call the original Daytona model with the Paul Newman Dial Rolex's worst-selling model at the time of its launch, especially if it was equipped with the distinctive white or black dial made by a subcontractor called Singer.

Even though James Cox possessed the watch that collectors had desperately sought for years, he kept this information to himself, although he probably knew that the old Rolex had become quite valuable over time.

He decided to submit it to Phillips at their auction house in New York, where the staff might have needed to rub their eyes before believing what they held in their hands. A Rolex with a Paul Newman Dial is valuable in itself, but this watch – Paul Newman's own watch, with its special inscription? The auction house estimated the watch's value at one million dollars (£775,000), and it's rare for a vintage watch auction to draw such a large audience. More than 700 people attended the auction in New York, with participants from 43 countries. The bidding started at $10 million and, after 12 intense minutes, the hammer fell on an offer from a phone bidder. This means Paul Newman's Rolex has once again vanished, as no one knows who placed the winning bid of $17,752,500 – or nearly £14 million.

This surpassed the previous record for a vintage watch by six million dollars (set by the sale of a Patek Philippe), making it the world's most expensive wristwatch.

The former owner, James Cox, donated a large portion of the proceeds from the sale to the Nell Newman Foundation – an organisation founded by Paul Newman's daughter that continues his legacy in education, animal welfare, and charitable causes. As for Paul Newman's Rolex? It remains uncertain whether we'll ever see it again, which ultimately adds to its legendary status...

> Paul Newman's own Rolex has long been the holy grail among watch collectors, but no one knew where it was until it suddenly appeared in New York

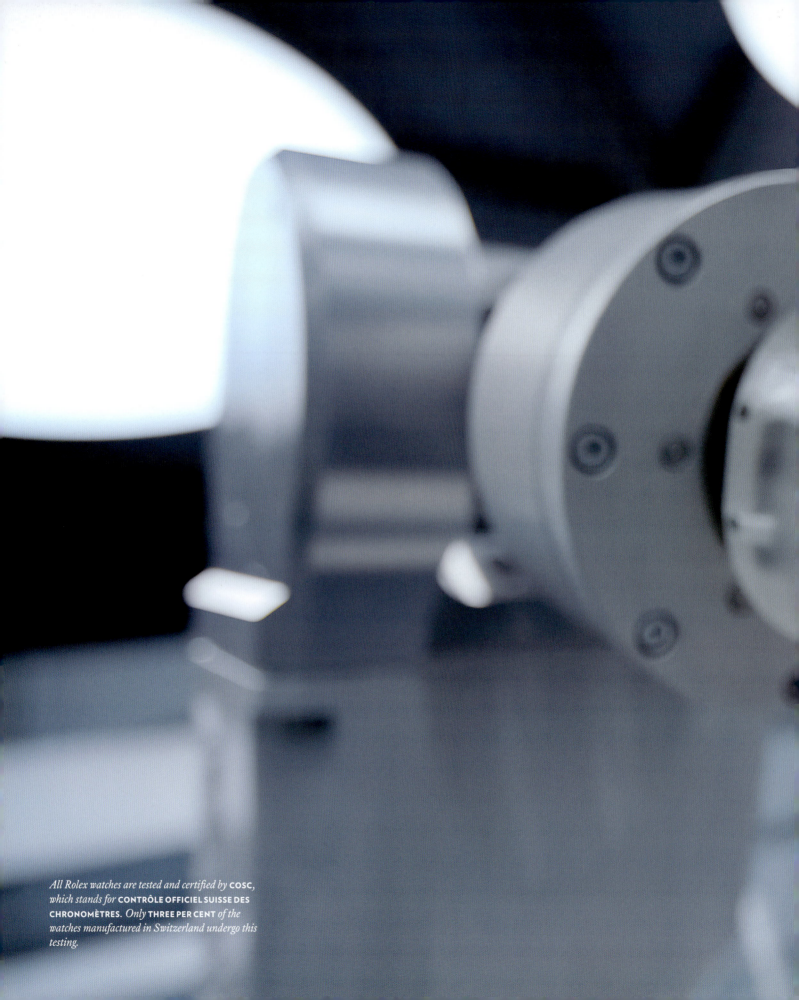

All Rolex watches are tested and certified by **COSC**, *which stands for* **CONTRÔLE OFFICIEL SUISSE DES CHRONOMÈTRES.** *Only* **THREE PER CENT** *of the watches manufactured in Switzerland undergo this testing.*

THE BOOK OF
ROLEX

EXPLORER

Even before the Explorer, created explicitly for harsh conditions on dangerous expeditions, mountaineers favoured the tough and reliable watches from Rolex

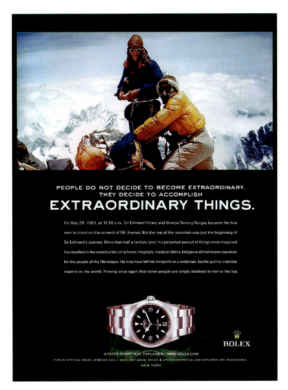

You can only do something for the first time **ONCE**, *and even today the* **EXPLORER** *is marketed with* **SIR EDMUND HILLARY'S** *greatest achievement, conquering* **MOUNT EVEREST** *with his faithful Sherpa,* **TENZING NORGAY**.

THE BOOK OF
ROLEX

An early **EXPLORER II** *from the 1970s when Rolex still used* **PLEXIGLASS**. *The raw* **NATO STRAP** *makes it absolutely* **PERFECT**.

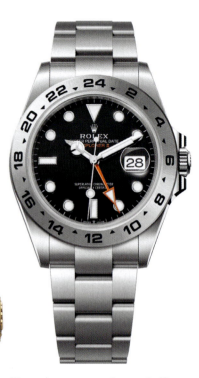

The **ROLEX EXPLORER II** *is recognised by its additional* **ORANGE HAND** *and the* **24-HOUR** *markings on the bezel, which help indicate whether it is 4 in the* **MORNING** *or the* **AFTERNOON**.

EXPLORER II REF. 16550 *from the 1970s, with a white dial. An* **ERROR** *in the paint used by Rolex sometimes causes the white to turn a* **CREAM COLOUR**, *and watches with this look are very sought after by* **COLLECTORS** *today.*

The **ROLEX EXPLORER** *is designed to be* **SIMPLE AND ROBUST** *without any frills. However, Rolex couldn't resist creating a version with* **GOLD ON THE CASE AND BRACELET**.

STEVE McQUEEN *is often associated with TAG Heuer's* **MONACO MODEL**, *which he wore in the film Le Mans. However, privately he wore a* **ROLEX EXPLORER** *on his wrist.*

THE BOOK OF
ROLEX

To the far left is the **ROLEX OYSTER** *worn by* **SIR EDMUND HILLARY** *when he conquered* **MOUNT EVEREST** *with* **TENZING NORGAY** *in May 1953. However, Rolex excels in marketing, and Hillary will forever be associated with the* **EXPLORER** *(to the right), even though the model was first introduced in* **1954**.

A mountaineer has the right gear because that's what you need when your office is a mountainside at an altitude of 8,000 metres. But in the 1930s, very few wristwatches could withstand extreme cold. One of the few was the Rolex Oyster, making it the natural choice for expeditions in the Himalayas, such as those by Hugh Ruttledge who, in 1933, had to turn back only 300 metres from the summit of Mount Everest.

The mountain was first conquered 20 years later by Sir Edmund Hillary who, along with his loyal Sherpa, Tenzing Norgay, reached the world's highest peak in 1953. Of course, they both wore a Rolex Oyster, and with their usual flair for marketing, Rolex launched the Explorer model that same year, linking the new watch with Hillary and Norgay's achievement. Clearly, it wasn't actually an Explorer they were wearing, but the model is still inseparably associated with the ascent of Mount Everest.

Since 1953, the Explorer model has been updated several times, incorporating the technical improvements that have gradually been introduced in all Rolex models. The design is minimalist, giving the watch a very clean look when viewed from a distance. However, Rolex haven't changed the basic shape, even though in 2010 the case grew from 36 to 39 millimetres, equipped with the robust Calibre 3132, which handles strong magnetic fields and large temperature fluctuations. In addition, the updated Explorer got a luminous blue coating on the hands and hour markers.

For collectors, however, nothing beats the classic Explorer models, preferably with a NATO strap as the final touch. The Explorer II is available with either a black or a white dial, but something went wrong with the paint Rolex used in the 1980s on Ref. 16550, and instead of the original white, the dial often takes on a yellowish hue. As always with Rolex, these small defects are the most sought after by collectors, and a vintage Explorer II with the yellowed dial can easily cost more than £11,000 today. An amusing detail is that things haven't gone much better with the black variant of Ref. 16550, where the paint often cracks, giving the dial a completely unique look.

The Explorer II came out in 1971 and is recognisable by the additional orange hand which, with the help of the bezel, can show whether it's 4 a.m. or 4 p.m., in case you find yourself at the North Pole or in a dark jungle. As with the Explorer, Rolex used daring expeditions to market the Explorer II, such as when Belgian Alain Hubert reached the North Pole on skis. His journey went from Siberia to Greenland in 106 days with little daylight and, naturally, Hubert had a Rolex Explorer II on his wrist. In 2011, the model turned 40 and, in connection with that, it received a major update, with the case growing from 40 to 42 millimetres.

The update also brought new, sturdier hands and the new Calibre 3187 with improved shock resistance. For added comfort, the Explorer II now features the Oyster bracelet with a seamless adjustment system and, to maintain the design, Rolex kept the fixed steel bezel, in contrast to many of their other models, where the bezel is now ceramic.

Both the Explorer and the Explorer II have in common that they are so-called 'tool watches' designed to fulfil a specific task in difficult conditions. You don't need to climb a mountain to own an Explorer, but it's nice to know that if you do, it won't be your watch that gives up along the way...

> Both the Explorer and the Explorer II are 'tool watches'. If you decide to climb a mountain, you can rest assured your watch won't let you down

THE BOOK OF
ROLEX

EDMUND HILLARY *and his faithful Sherpa,* **TENZING NORGAY.** *Together they reached the summit of* **EVEREST** *on 29 May 1953.* **TENZING NORGAY'S** *date of birth was unknown, so after the expedition he decided that this date would be his* **BIRTHDAY** *from then on.*

THE FIRST EXPLORER

Simple, elegant and, most importantly, robust – the **ROLEX OYSTER** *was one of the few* **WATCHES** *that could withstand the gruelling conditions in the mountains, and Rolex took these qualities and made them even better with the* **EXPLORER SERIES.**

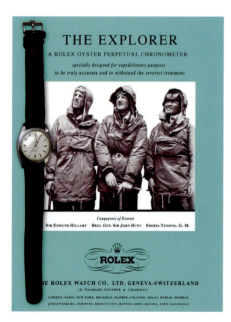

ROLEX *were always the masters of advertising. This advert for the* **OYSTER PERPETUAL** *shows* **HILLARY, HUNT** *and* **NORGAY,** *after conquering* **EVEREST.** *It was an effective way to market the* **EXPLORER** *as the watch for, well, explorers.*

THE BOOK OF ROLEX

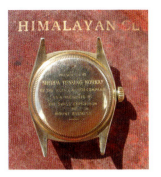

The back of the gold watch that **ROLEX** *presented to* **TENZING NORGAY** *after conquering Everest. Note that they spelled his name* **NORKAY**.

An early **EXPLORER** *with a leather strap whose hands and markings have turned a yellow colour. For a* **COLLECTOR**, *a watch like this is a dream come true.*

THE FIRST EXPLORER II

EXPLORER II *had more functions than the* **EXPLORER**. *For instance, the extra hand, which takes* **24 HOURS** *to make a full rotation, and the* **DATE**. *Rolex introduced the world's first* **WRISTWATCH** *with the date displayed like this in 1945 with the* **DATEJUST SERIES**.

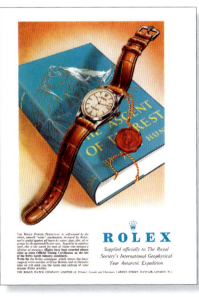

An advert for the **OYSTER PERPETUAL** *together with* **JOHN HUNT'S** *book about the climbing of* **MOUNT EVEREST**, *which was a bestseller in its day.*

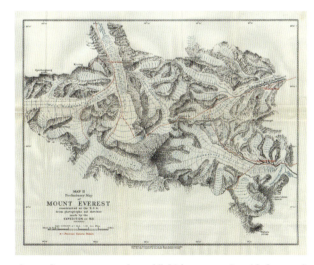

A map of **MOUNT EVEREST**, *the world's highest mountain, with the summit some* **8,850 METRES** *above sea level.* **6,600 PEOPLE** *have tried to conquer Everest since then.* **MORE THAN 300** *have lost their lives in the process.*

41

*The **EXPLORER** utilises a special technology for readability in the dark called **CHROMALIGHT**, developed by Rolex. Both the hands receive a distinctive luminescent treatment, emitting a blue glow that lasts **TWICE AS LONG** as traditional phosphorescent materials.*

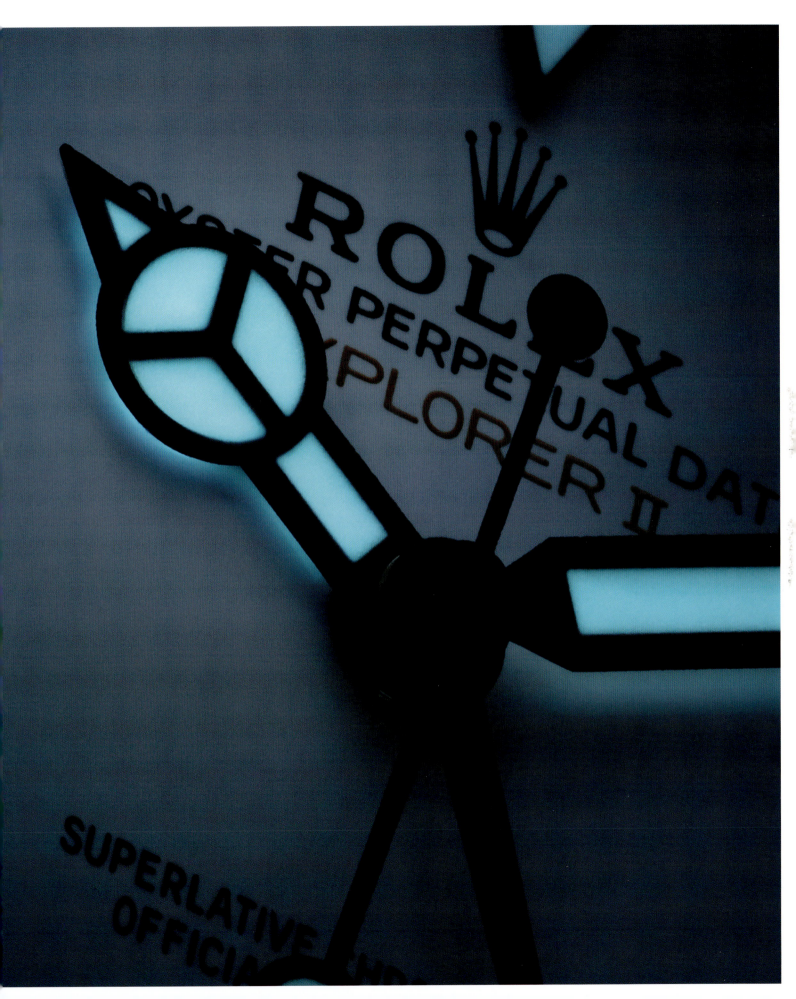

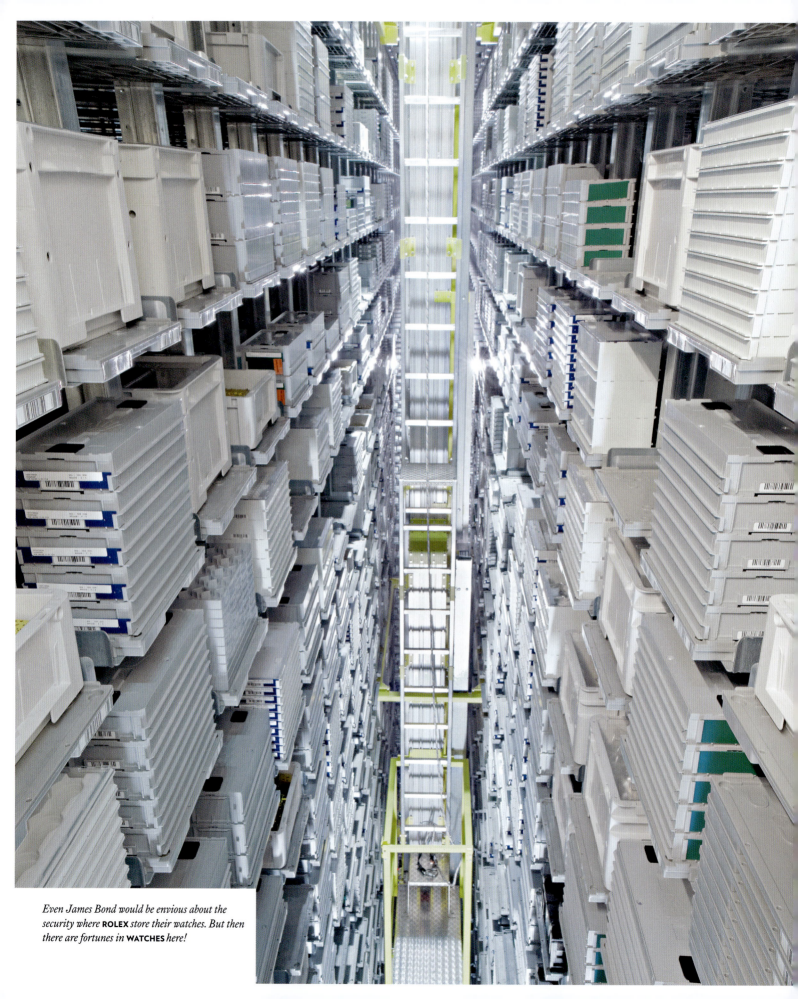

*Even James Bond would be envious about the security where **ROLEX** store their watches. But then there are fortunes in **WATCHES** here!*

THE BOOK OF
ROLEX

A ROLEX IS 100 PER CENT
SWISS-MADE

A Rolex isn't just 100 per cent Swiss-made — it's made 100 per cent by Rolex in four specialised factories around Switzerland, complete with their own foundry

Only 60 per cent of a watch needs to be manufactured in Switzerland before it can be called 'Swiss-Made'. However, every part of a Rolex is manufactured in Switzerland, and Rolex makes every part. Hans Wilsdorf, Rolex's founder, started his business in London under the name of Wilsdorf & Davis, importing Swiss watch movements. By the time Rolex started manufacturing its own movements, they did so in Bienne, Switzerland.

To manufacture a Rolex is a time-consuming process, and on average it takes a year from start to finish. The work is done by Rolex's 6,000 employees at four different factories, where watchmaking traditions meet the latest technology. Rolex like to point out that the reason they produce every part themselves is because it's the only way to ensure every part lives up to 'our own impossible standards'.

It wasn't always like that, but 50 years ago the company started acquiring those suppliers who did most of their business with Rolex SA. Financially, it made perfect sense to control every part of the production, but the logistics was a bit more complex. At one point Rolex had 20 different production facilities at various locations in Switzerland. Needless to say, the delivery of parts took up far too many resources, so in the early 1990s Rolex started to reduce the number of production sites. Not just to have a leaner production, but also to improve quality and increase research in new materials.

Since 2013 production has been taking place in four highly specialised facilities. The watch movements

have always been assembled in Bienne by 2,000 highly trained employees. The demand for quality is extreme, but then it needs to be, because every single watch movement is sent for certification by COSC, and for Rolex, a success rate of less than 100 per cent would be nothing short of a disaster. So far, the factory in Bienne has delivered just that.

In his memoirs, Hans Wilsdorf explains how the production of the watch movements was always left to Bienne, but everything else was manufactured in Geneva, being influenced by the city's inhabitants, who have a unique and sophisticated taste when it comes to watches.

Product development, design and production take place at Rolex headquarters in Les Acacias in Geneva, and components from the three other production facilities all end up here. Plan-les-Ouates, also in Geneva, produces the watchcases and bracelets. This is also where you find the Rolex foundry, which makes the 18-carat gold used by Rolex, including the unique Everose gold. This is actually red gold combined with platinum. Not only does Everose gold have an extremely hard surface that is scratch-resistant, but the platinum also helps preserve the distinctive pink colour. The last facility is located in Chêne-Bourg, and produces the dials for every Rolex, as well as selecting the diamonds and precious gems.

> Rolex never reveal production figures, but COSC will tell you how many watch movements they certify every year and from which manufacturers

Rolex never reveal their production figures, but every year COSC records how many watch movements they have certified and from which manufacturers. In 2014 they certified an amazing 750,000 watch movements from Rolex.

OYSTER PERPETUAL *is much more than just Rolex's* **ENTRY-LEVEL MODEL.** *It may not be as spectacular as the Daytona, but the details exude* **PERFECTION.**

THE BOOK OF
ROLEX

THE CLASSIC
OYSTER

The Oyster Perpetual is Rolex's entry-level model and has a unique simplistic style – the story of Rolex begins with the Oyster series

*It's a popular **MISCONCEPTION** that Rolex invented the **AUTOMATIC** watch movement. What they did was improve the invention, placing the movement inside the world's first **WATERPROOF** wristwatch, and the **OYSTER SERIES** was born.*

THE BOOK OF
ROLEX

If you're not into the **COLOURFUL VERSIONS**, *the Oyster Perpetual can still be the epitome of* **CONSERVATIVE ELEGANCE.**

In the past, the **SMALLEST** *Oyster model was just* **26 MILLIMETRES**, *but that was considered too small, so now it has been increased to* **28 MILLIMETRES**.

'**ALL THAT GLITTERS IS NOT GOLD**', *for your Oyster is only available in* **STEEL**. *If you want other materials, you'll have to move up in the* **ROLEX HIERARCHY.**

The **BUBBLY** *Oyster was a novelty in 2024, combining the colourful editions launched in 2020. Rolex enjoy being* **UNPREDICTABLE.**

The Oyster models are now available in **28, 31, 34, 36 AND 41 MILLIMETRES**. *The two largest sizes are recognised by the double hour markers at* **3, 6 AND 9 O'CLOCK.**

THE BOOK OF
ROLEX

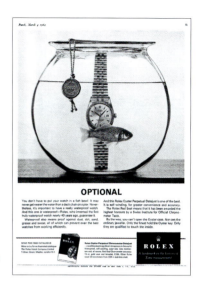

Look, a Rolex is **WATERPROOF**! *Customers didn't quite understand what Rolex meant, so dealers demonstrated it by placing an* **AQUARIUM** *in the shop window –* **WITH A GOLDFISH AND A ROLEX OYSTER**.

The Oyster Perpetual is without luxury and only available in steel. It is Rolex's most affordable model and the gateway to the Rolex universe. Rolex are not known for doing things by halves, and the Oyster Perpetual is not about just a few models. The line-up is incredibly broad, and not intended to be a series of watches designed to lure customers into the store only to upsell them a much more expensive model. It is a fully-fledged member of the Rolex family, available in sizes ranging from 28 to 41 millimetres, proving that Rolex maintain their commitment to the classic models that laid the foundation for their success.

The Oyster was the world's first waterproof watch, a quality demonstrated by swimmer Mercedes Gleitze when she became the first British woman to swim the English Channel in just over 15 hours. Naturally, the Oyster Perpetual she wore throughout performed exactly as expected.

A waterproof watch was quite a novel concept back then, and it took some time to explain it to customers. To get the message across, Rolex instructed their dealers to get a bowl, fill it with goldfish, place the new watch at the bottom, and display the whole set-up in the shop window. One dealer went further and arranged for a well-dressed young lady to sit in the window with an Oyster Perpetual on her wrist, occasionally submerging the watch, presumably to the ever-increasing puzzlement of the goldfish. The initiative seems to have worked, as the Oyster models became the backbone of Rolex's success. They not only crossed the English Channel but also reached the summit of Mount Everest with Sir Edmund Hillary. And it was from the Oyster series that Rolex developed the Explorer and the successful Submariner, Rolex's first true divers' watch and the first waterproof wristwatch capable of withstanding a depth of 100 metres.

Today, the Oyster Perpetual is available with two different movements depending on the size of the case. The 28, 31 and 34-millimetre models are equipped with Calibre 2232, while the 36 and 41-millimetre models use Calibre 3230. The larger 41-millimetre model reflects Rolex's commitment to keeping the Oyster Perpetual series modern.

Rolex did not invent the self-winding watch, but they further developed the invention so that the rotor could rotate through 360 degrees. This meant that the watch stored more energy and became more reliable, even if you were swimming across the English Channel.

> Rolex's dealers were told to get a goldfish bowl, put the new waterproof Oyster model at the bottom, and place it in their display window

THE BOOK OF
ROLEX

Even the best **IDEAS** *need to mature, which includes the shape of the Rolex* **WATCHCASE**. *This one was called* **THE OCTAGONAL**, *and didn't really work.*

The **ROUNDED** *shape was better, like this model from the 1920s. The famous trademark Rolex* **CROWN** *is still missing. This detail was yet to be introduced.*

The **SECONDS HAND** *was fully integrated once the Oyster* **BECAME AN OFFICIALLY CERTIFIED CHRONOMETER**, *another feature in which Rolex would lead the way.*

THE WATCHCASE *has found its form, and is equipped with the* **LUGS** *that all Rolex watches have to this day, along with the* **AUTOMATIC MOVEMENT**.

OYSTER-QUARTZ? *Yes, when the first quartz movements emerged, even Rolex believed it was* **THE FUTURE**, *but fortunately, the idea was abandoned after* **A FEW YEARS**…

THE BOOK OF
ROLEX

*An **OYSTER** model from 2017. Today, the Roman numerals have **DISAPPEARED**, so there are no longer distinct ladies' and men's models. Oyster Perpetual has become **UNISEX**.*

IN THE PAST, *the Oyster Perpetual came in a **26-MILLIMETRE** size like this one, but today even women wear **LARGER WATCHES**.*

*Oyster Perpetual from **2024** - it clearly shows the heritage from **ROLEX'S FIRST MODELS**. Elegant without unnecessary frills, but the quality is **UNMISTAKABLE**.*

*The **OYSTER PERPETUAL** is much more than just Rolex's most **AFFORDABLE MODEL**. The heart is the Calibre 3230, which led to the filing of several patents and which is also used in models like Submariner and Sea-Dweller.*

Every Rolex has its own **UNIQUE** *features, but your* **AUTHORISED** *Rolex dealer knows all of them. This also means you can have your Rolex serviced* **IN ALL CORNERS OF THE WORLD.**

THE BOOK OF
ROLEX

WHEN YOUR ROLEX NEEDS
SERVICING

If you want your Rolex to last forever, you need to have it serviced, typically every seven years. But when you get it back, it's like receiving a brand new watch

YOU GET SERVICE WITH A ROLEX

*All parts of the watch are **DISMANTLED AND CLEANED**, from the bezel to the **MOVEMENT** itself, which consists of **HUNDREDS OF PARTS**.*

*After the watch is dismantled it needs to be **POLISHED**, a tricky process that requires special training in order to handle the various metals such as steel and **DIFFERENT KINDS OF GOLD**.*

*After being polished the movement is **LUBRICATED** with up to five different kinds of oil. At the same time, up to seven different **GASKETS** are replaced.*

*When the watchcase is **REASSEMBLED**, it's time to check that your watch is still **WATERPROOF**. Then the movement goes back into the watchcase, before being adjusted after a **VERIFICATION PROCESS**.*

Polishing a ROLEX requires skill and experience to avoid damaging precious materials like STEEL, GOLD OR PLATINUM. The bracelet itself is covered with a PROTECTIVE FILM developed for each specific model, and the polishing is carried out as a series of steps.

THE BOOK OF
ROLEX

Rolex's **AUTHORISED DEALERS** *are the only ones who can service your watch correctly, since they have the tools and experience. Just as you would with an expensive car, if you should one day put your watch up* **FOR SALE**, *the new owner might well ask you to document the* **SERVICE HISTORY**.

Some might think that servicing a Rolex is a bit costly. It can only be done by an authorised dealer and typically costs around £600 ($750) on a popular model like the Submariner. But then it only seems expensive until you know how much work goes into keeping your watch in perfect condition.

Your watch is literally taken apart, and every single part is cleaned, checked and lubricated. Vital parts, such as the crown, are replaced, and finally the watchcase and bracelet are polished until they look as good as new. Polishing a Rolex is an extensive operation that requires skill and experience, regardless of whether the watch is steel, gold or platinum. Before even getting close to polishing a Rolex, special training is given at the factory in Switzerland where continual improvements and developments to the machines used help to get the right shine and the sharp edges on the watchcase.

Rolex recommend that their watches are serviced every five to seven years. Some owners only service their watches every ten years, which usually isn't a problem, because a Rolex is among the sturdiest watches in the world. But if the watch is never serviced then the movement will eventually be damaged from a lack of lubrication, just like a car would be. Service your watch, and it'll literally last forever.

Every Rolex dealer will from time to time receive watches that haven't been serviced in decades, having been stored or just forgotten. In most cases, it's possible to get the watch going again, but often a lot of parts need to be replaced, which can be expensive.

To claim that Rolex are conservative is the understatement of the century. New models evolve at a glacier-like pace, but when they do happen, you can be sure they will have been thoroughly tried and tested. This is because Rolex exist in a world of their own, and when a new model does come along, it's often an evolution of what has gone before. The famous brand from Switzerland will never follow trends, but will simply do what they do best – constantly evolve what is probably the world's best-known Swiss watch.

That means that a Rolex GMT-Master from 1995 essentially is the same as a Rolex GMT-Master from 2015, apart from any minor updates and improvements. They are based on a proven and thoroughly developed technology, but they still need servicing if they are to function well. Having the watch serviced can also detect problems that could prove costly if left unnoticed. A crack in the sapphire glass can be impossible to detect with the naked eye, but over time it can develop into a serious problem. The Submariner uses five different lubricants for all the parts to function, and an equal number of rubber gaskets, which eventually will dry out if they are not replaced. If this happens, water can leak into the movement, making it very expensive to get your watch back in order.

A great advantage to owning a Rolex is that parts are always available if and when they become worn out. Rolex guarantee that parts will be available for up to 30 years after a model is taken out of production. Most of the time this means that you can get parts up to 35 years after a particular model has left production. If you intend to pass on your watch to the next generation, this is a very important feature.

> **It typically costs around £600 ($750) to service a Rolex. This only seems expensive until you know how much work goes into keeping your watch in perfect condition**

When your Rolex goes into **SERVICE**, *it'll literally get stripped down. In a process that takes several days it will be cleaned and* **ALL PARTS TESTED**. *When it is returned to you by Rolex, it is virtually a* **BRAND NEW WATCH**.

THE BOOK OF ROLEX

1

YOUR WATCH IS STRIPPED DOWN

When your watch is being serviced, it will pass through a number of sequences, perfected through a century and millions of watches. However, the majority of it still takes place in the hands of experienced watchmakers, although advanced machines are also used where they improve quality. But before the work can begin, the watch needs to be stripped down and all the little bits and pieces placed in a special bowl that serves as a home for the watch while it is being serviced. A Rolex Submariner, for example, consists of 220 individual parts.

2

EVALUATION

The watchmaker will then make a note of the serial number of the watch, and do a general assessment of the condition of the watch. This means the quality of vital elements like the glass dial, bracelet and, most importantly, the movement. This is also done so that it's possible to warn the owner if any vital parts need to be replaced.

3

VITAL DATA IS SENT TO ROLEX

The most important data about your watch is sent to Rolex in Switzerland, providing the factory with vital information about the performance of their products over time. Then all parts of your watch need to be cleaned thoroughly, which is done in five different liquids, dissolving dust, grease, and anything else that might have made its way into your watch.

4

POLISHING

Polishing a Rolex to the perfect shine requires a high degree of precision. No one is allowed to operate the polishing machines without training at Rolex in Switzerland, and then they have to prove themselves polishing the watchcases and bracelets in steel, before moving on to the models in gold and other precious metals.

5

LAPPING

The lapping machine is a new invention, developed to preserve the sharp edges on the watchcase. Vintage models often have soft edges because they were polished before lapping was introduced. Normally a Rolex is polished so it's 98 per cent as it was when it was new. Some owners wish to maintain the worn look, so they choose not to have their watches polished.

6

SCRATCHES ARE REPAIRED

It is now possible to repair big dents and scratches in the watchcase or bracelet. Previously, dents had to be polished away, removing a lot of material in the process, but now it's possible to fill the gap with steel or gold. A laser will inject material into the dent, more or less as you would when filling a tooth. Then the surface is polished, making the repair invisible. After polishing, the watchcase and bracelet are cleaned using steam and ultrasound.

7

THE HEART OF YOUR WATCH

After polishing, it's time for the watch movement itself. First, all parts are examined for wear and, if necessary, worn-down parts are replaced. It's a time-consuming process, all done by hand, following a number of complex procedures. Along the way the various parts of the watch are lubricated. The number of lubricants used depends on the model. The Rolex Deepsea requires five different lubricants, and seven new gaskets to be fitted.

8

PUTTING THE PARTS BACK IN THE BOX

When the watch movement is reassembled, it is once again fitted to the watchcase along with the hands and dial. When this process is complete, the watchmaker issues a service certificate with a two-year warranty.

9

CERTIFICATION

Now the watch is ready to go through a certification process to ensure that it lives up to Rolex's standards for precision. Also, the watchmaker will verify that the watch is still waterproof. This is done with the movement removed, to protect against leaks. The watchcase is tested in a vacuum and then in a pressure chamber to ensure that it can be worn to the specified depth – 100 metres below the surface, in the case of the Submariner. Then the watch is placed in a chamber heated to 45°C for five minutes, before being placed in a special refrigerator at a temperature of 5°C. After this, there shouldn't be any condensation on the inside of the sapphire glass.

10

SIMULATOR TEST

Finally, the watch is electronically tested, to ensure it lives up to the chronometer certification. Then the watch goes onto a simulator that mimics the movements of the hands for 72 hours. The precision is measured once again, before the watch is ready for its owner.

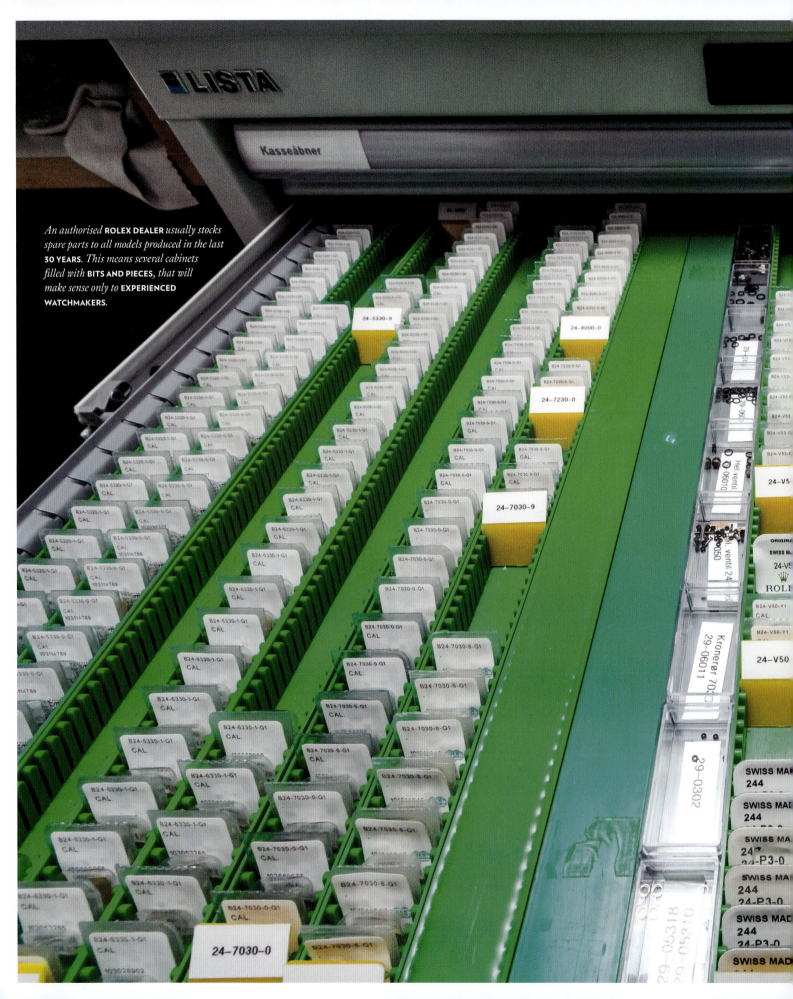

An authorised **ROLEX DEALER** *usually stocks spare parts to all models produced in the last* **30 YEARS**. *This means several cabinets filled with* **BITS AND PIECES**, *that will make sense only to* **EXPERIENCED WATCHMAKERS.**

The Datejust in Rolesor, Rolex's combination of **WHITE GOLD AND STEEL**, *equipped with the exclusive* **JUBILEE BRACELET**, *is an incredibly elegant* **COMBINATION**.

THE BOOK OF
ROLEX

THE CLASSIC ROLEX
DATEJUST

The Datejust was introduced in 1945, and has been part of the Rolex line-up ever since. It can be conservative, flamboyant or even outrageous – but it's always elegant

The first **DATEJUST** *was the first watch in the world that displayed the date in a* **WINDOW**, *which has since become the standard. It really is the classic Rolex model, having been in production for more than* **70 YEARS**.

THE BOOK OF
ROLEX

*The **SMALLEST** version of the Datejust is just 31 millimetres. **SOPHIA LOREN** would not go wrong with this version.*

*The **MEDIUM-SIZED** Datejust is 36 millimetres, which was considered a **MEN'S WATCH** over **70 YEARS AGO** when the model was introduced.*

CONSERVATIVE *is good, conservative works, like the Datejust in* **ROLESOR** *with an Oysterclasp bracelet.* **UNDERSTATED** *and elegant, but you are never in doubt that it is* **EXCLUSIVE**.

*It doesn't get **SIMPLER** than this Datejust, but on the next pages, you can see what else the model **HAS TO OFFER**!*

*This one should be called **RICHARD GERE**, because it was actually this model of **DATEJUST** that he wore when he starred with Julia Roberts in **PRETTY WOMAN**.*

THE BOOK OF
ROLEX

DATEJUST *has been in continuous production for 70 years and it is still Rolex's most* **POPULAR** *model. It has graced the wrists of celebrities such as tennis ace* **CAROLINE WOZNIACKI**, *Leonardo DiCaprio's crazy stockbroker in* **THE WOLF OF WALL STREET** *and American president* **DWIGHT D. EISENHOWER.**

Datejust is elegant, classic and sporty all at the same time, which explains why it has been Rolex's most popular model for as long as anyone can remember. We will never know how many Datejusts have been produced, because Rolex don't give out that information, but after 70 years, it must be quite a few. For this reason, the Rolex dealers always keep plenty of models in stock.

The Datejust series was first introduced in 1945, and through the years it's been continuously updated. In fact, Datejust was introduced in the very same year Rolex celebrated its 40th anniversary, which was also marked with the introduction of the Jubilee bracelet. So this really is one of Rolex's classic models, and one which combines all of the brand's best qualities. A Datejust is functional and understated, but there's no mistaking the elegance and quality that are visible in every part of the watch.

The owners of Datejusts are known to replace the watch dial at some point, and there are more than 100 different dials to choose from. Another great advantage is that when you replace the Datejust dial, you get to keep the old dial, so it's possible to bring the watch back to its original condition.

Datejust wasn't the first watch to display the date, but prior to this it was indicated by a small hand that would change once a day. On the Datejust the date was placed at three o'clock, which is an idea that has been widely copied ever since. You still have to adjust the date in months just 30 days long. The date is also placed under a small magnifying glass that Rolex call 'the Cyclops lens'. These days the invention has become a trademark for most Rolex models, but it was first seen on Datejust. Incidentally, it's also one of the tell-tale signs when spotting a fake Rolex, since the imitated Cyclops lens doesn't enlarge the date. The way the date changes was improved in 1956, and these days it changes in the blink of an eye.

You can still have your Datejust in steel, and this is believed to be Rolex's single most popular model because it looks like white gold, especially when new or recently polished. It has the smooth bezel, whereas the ripped bezel is exclusively for the three gold versions. Rolex manufacture their own gold, known as Rolesor, which is a combination of 18-carat gold and steel; it gives a tougher surface that keeps the special glow from the gold and is better at resisting scratches. Need a bit more bling? Well, you can add diamonds, or emeralds, like on the new Pearlmaster.

The classic Datejust has maintained the original size of 36 millimetres. This used to be the standard size for a man's watch, but fashion has changed. Men's watches are usually around 40 millimetres today, and women mostly purchase the 36-millimetre version. In 2009 Rolex introduced the Datejust II in 41 millimetres with a series of new watch dials. The design has simply been enlarged from the original Datejust, so the two look similar.

Just like the original Datejust, the Datejust II is waterproof to depths of 100 metres, uses the Rolex Calibre 3116 and is delivered exclusively with the Oyster bracelet. The original Datejust is still available, underlining the exclusivity of the Datejust series.

> We will never know how many Datejusts have been produced, since Rolex don't give out that information, but after 70 years it has to be quite a few

THE BOOK OF ROLEX

DATEJUST PEARLMASTER *was introduced in 2015 and shows the wide range of the series, with a bit of* **GOLD AND SOME EMERALDS.**

Rolex is often the very definition of **CONSERVATIVE** *but the Datejust is where the designer is allowed to be* **PLAYFUL.**

THE BOOK OF
ROLEX

The **PEARLMASTER**. *With a size of just* **39 MILLIMETRES**, *the original Datejust appeals to both men and* **WOMEN**.

To change the watchface on your **DATEJUST** *is quite popular. There are more than* **100 DIALS** *to choose from, and you get to keep the old one.*

GOLD, **BLACK DIAL** *and* **DIAMONDS** – *another variation on the Datejust, and Rolex often introduce special versions produced in* **LIMITED NUMBERS**.

Pretty in pink? Okay, so **ROSE-TINTED LEATHER** *and* **DIAMONDS** *is not for the gentleman, but the Datejust is* **POPULAR** *among women.*

*The first **AIR-KING** came out in 1958. The model has **CHANGED** over the years, but for many, this is still **THEIR FIRST ROLEX**.*

THE PILOT'S WATCH
AIR-KING

The Rolex Air series was launched in 1945, at the height of WWII, and today the Air-King is the last Air model still in production

It wasn't just **PILOTS** *who wore an Air-King; evidently,* **SPIES** *did too. Here, they also promoted the special* **TWINLOCK SCREW-DOWN CROWN** *– and it could be yours for just* **33 BRITISH POUNDS**!

*In 2014, the Air-King was **REMOVED** from Rolex's line-up, but in **2016**, it made a comeback in an entirely new version with a **40-MILLIMETRE** case and without **CROWN GUARDS**, as seen here, which many collectors **PREFER**.*

THE BOOK OF
ROLEX

Notice the so-called **CROWN GUARDS** *on the latest Air-King, which are different from the* **2016 MODEL**. *In the middle, an advertisement for the new* **AIR-KING** *from Rolex. And of course, a classic watch must also have an* **AMBASSADOR**, *which Air-King has found in the form of singer* **MICHAEL BUBLÉ**.

In 1945 Rolex launched several special models as a tribute to the Royal Air Force pilots who fought in the Battle of Britain and gave them all names containing the word 'Air' – such as Air-King, Air-Giant, Air-Tiger, and so on. The models were very popular, not least because of Rolex's efforts during the war, when they delivered thousands of watches to British officers who were prisoners of war in Germany.

Additionally, there was a great need for robust and reliable wristwatches – remember that a Rolex watch played a significant part in the plan for what later became known as the Great Escape. The Air-King was created specifically for pilots who needed a simple and reliable watch that would function under all conditions, and that's exactly what Rolex provided them with. The fact that the model is still in production 80 years later says it all, and it remains one of the most affordable Rolexes you can buy. One of the key features of the Air-King then as now was Rolex's waterproof Oyster case, which was also resistant to pressure; invaluable for the pilots flying the bombers. When they reached their maximum altitude, many watches would either stop or begin to run incorrectly, but not the Rolex Air-King.

The Oyster case was launched in 1926 for the first waterproof wristwatch, and the key was Rolex's patented Twinlock system, where the crown and the watch mechanism were in two sealed zones.

The name itself came from the striking resemblance of the watch mechanism to an oyster when the crown was screwed down. When this 'oyster' sealed around the watch mechanism, it was not only waterproof to 100 metres but also able to withstand both cold and pressure. An Air-King was on board the first flight over Mount Everest, known as the Houston Expedition, and when pilots Owen Cathcart-Jones and Ken Waller set their record by flying from London to Melbourne in the world's first commercial jet aircraft, the De Havilland Comet, faster than anyone had done before, they used a Rolex Air-King as their onboard chronometer. Like Rolex's other 'tool watches', the Air-King is made of 904L stainless steel, a popular material in the aerospace and aviation industries. It is extremely resistant to corrosion and can be polished to a perfect finish.

In 1958, Rolex developed a series of wristwatches under the name Air-King, before the designation disappeared in 2014, and since 2016 it has been a distinct series, only available with a black dial, a green seconds hand, and the 'Air-King' inscription in the same lettering style as when the watch was first launched in the 1950s.

There have been several different movements in the Air-King models, but the current version uses the Calibre 3230, which includes approximately 70 hours of power reserve and is, of course, certified as a Superlative Chronometer. As always with Rolex, it is beautifully executed, even though only your watchmaker will ever see its internal craftsmanship. The design also has its own story. The dial features markers for 3, 6 and 9, as well as clear seconds markers to optimise the chronometer function. A design element introduced in 2022 is the so-called crown guards, which previous models did not have. Additionally, Rolex uses its special green colour for the seconds hand and the 'Rolex' marking on the dial.

As with all Rolex models, the Air-King has its own unique history. Hans Wilsdorf, who founded Rolex, wanted a watch that could be sold at a reasonable price to ensure that the soldiers and pilots who needed them could afford to buy them. And they could with a Rolex Air-King.

> The Air-King is Rolex's most affordable model because Hans Wilsdorf, the founder of Rolex, wanted to create a watch at a reasonable price so that soldiers and pilots could afford to buy them

THE CROWN *is just one of many components manufactured by* **ROLEX**. *In fact, every part of your Rolex is manufactured in* **SWITZERLAND**.

MATERIALS

With the exception of raw materials like steel, Rolex have no suppliers and even have their own foundry to ensure every single part is of optimum quality

NO SUPPLIER IS GOOD ENOUGH
Rolex produce every bit of their watches themselves. It's the only way to guarantee that the finished product meets the company's extreme demands on quality. It's certainly possible to find a more complex and sophisticated watch than a Rolex, but no one combines quality and reliability in the same way.

A SPECIAL TYPE OF STEEL
Rolex use a special kind of steel for their watches. Most watches are produced in a steel alloy called 316L, as did Rolex until 1958. But when Sea-Dweller was introduced it was produced in a steel alloy called 904L, and today this is used in all watches manufactured by Rolex. The advantage is that 904L has an extremely hard surface that's almost impossible to scratch or dent. However, this very quality also makes it extremely tough to work with. But because Rolex produce around one million watches every year, it made sense to invest in developing special machine tools to handle 904L steel.

ROLEX HAVE THEIR OWN FOUNDRY
Rolex produce all their gold and platinum in-house. They buy in 24-carat gold and the foundry turns it into gold, white gold and the unique Everose gold – Rolex's version of red gold which contains both bronze and platinum. Unlike normal red gold, Everose doesn't lose its unique tint, and thanks to the platinum, it has a much harder surface that resists scratches well.

DEVELOPING NEW MATERIALS
Everose quickly became fashionable, and gives Rolex an advantage over the competition. But the company has developed new materials like this since the 1930s. Rolesor, a combination of steel and gold, was introduced in 1933, and is used on a number of models today along with White Rolesor, a combination of white gold and steel.

ROLEX BUY THEIR OWN PRECIOUS STONES
In the last 100 years Rolex have purchased around 20 million diamonds, and so far only two have been fakes. Rolex have an entire department employing what are probably the world's finest experts in precious stones. They buy in the diamonds and emeralds for the watches, and Rolex have even developed a unique way to attach the diamonds, that even the most skilled manufacturers of fake watches can't duplicate.

USING CERAMICS
The bezel is where a watch will often become scratched. Since 2005 the bezel on many Rolex models has been manufactured in Cerachrom, a ceramic material that has been hardened at 1,600 °C and is extremely durable. At first Cerachrom was only available in black, but now it's possible to add colour, like the classic red and blue 'Pepsi' bezel on the GMT-Master.

PLATINUM IS THE ULTIMATE
Platinum is the ultimate material for Rolex's absolute top models. It exhibits contradictory properties: it is hard and incredibly dense, yet difficult to work with and extremely challenging to polish. Therefore, servicing a platinum watch must always be done at Rolex in Switzerland. Another material used is titanium, with, for example, the Yacht-Master available in a titanium version.

THE WORLD'S TOUGHEST GLASS
Rolex manufacture the sapphire glass with the so-called 'Cyclops lens' that enlarges the date ×2.5. This feature was first seen on the Datejust in 1953, but today it's used on all models except the Sea-Dweller. Sapphire glass is almost unbreakable and has a superior clarity. Over the years the manufacturing methods have been continuously developed, and in the later Rolex models the Cyclops lens has received a special anti-glare treatment.

THE BOOK OF ROLEX

A selection of BRACELETS from Rolex. Some models come with several different bracelets. Taking a moment to choose the right one can make a significant DIFFERENCE.

THE BRACELET

Vintage models are often seen on a leather bracelet or NATO strap, but if you wear a Rolex, chances are it sits around your wrist with a gold or steel bracelet

OYSTER BRACELET

It was introduced in the late 1930s and has been continuously developed since then. It's mostly used on the sports models, but also on certain classic models like Datejust. It can be combined with a number of clasps such as Oysterlock and Oysterclasp, and even Easylink which can be continuously adjusted. This is a great advantage since you can tighten the bracelet, for instance when doing sports.

JUBILEE BRACELET

A very elegant five-link bracelet which fits comfortably even around smaller wrists. It was launched in 1945, the same year Rolex celebrated its 40th anniversary. It's always fitted with the Crownclasp, Rolex's elegant concealed clasp.

PRESIDENT BRACELET

The three-link bracelet can be recognised by its rounded links. It was introduced in 1956 on the exclusive Day-Date series. Even today the President bracelet only comes with the gold versions of the Day-Date and Day-Date II. The President bracelet always comes with a concealed clasp.

PEARLMASTER BRACELET

Elegant and feminine, it was introduced in 1992 with the then-new Pearlmaster series. It is made up of larger links that are joined together like you would a piece of precious jewellery, which ensures comfort for the wearer, even when the watch doesn't fit tightly around the wrist.

OYSTERFLEX BRACELET

This latest link bracelet is a clear indication that although Rolex are extremely conservative, they never stop developing products and finding original solutions. Oysterflex combines the comfort of the soft rubber strap with strength and stability. Inside the rubber strap is a titanium and nickel core. The Oysterflex is, to date, only available on the Yacht-Master in Everose.

OYSTERLOCK

The part of your watch that is subjected to the most use is the clasp on the bracelet. It's also the most critical part, because if it fails, you could lose your watch. Rolex's most popular clasp is the Oysterlock, debuting in 2005 after years of rigorous testing and development. Even the sound it makes when you open and close your watch, has been carefully tuned. Rolex state that the clasp and bracelet are engineered to be opened and closed around 300,000 times.

EASYLINK

A watch needs to be comfortable, and Easylink makes it possible to extend or tighten the bracelet in 5-millimetre increments, for instance, when travelling. When the temperature rises, your watch can start to tighten around your wrist. If the temperature drops, your watch can get too loose. With Easylink you can adjust this in a second.

GLIDELOCK

Glidelock makes it possible to extend the bracelet by 20 millimetres in 2-millimetre increments. This is ideal if you need to wear a wetsuit, and explains why this feature is found on diving watches like the Submariner and the Sea-Dweller. The Deepsea has a special version of Glidelock where you can adjust the bracelet while still wearing the watch.

FLIPLOCK

Fliplock is a small link that extends from the bracelet. This way you can expand the bracelet on the Deepsea and the Sea-Dweller by up to 26 millimetres. When Glidelock and Fliplock are combined, it's possible to wear a diving suit with a thickness of 7 millimetres.

<small>THE BOOK OF</small>

ROLEX

THE MOVEMENT

The heart of your Rolex is a small mechanical miracle, created with magnificent precision and developed over more than a century, and yet, you might never see it

Movement or calibre, it may go by different names, but it relates to the same thing – the heart of your watch. Unlike other watch manufacturers, Rolex only introduce a new movement every 30 years or so. It is actually a miraculous piece of precision engineering, which is why many fine watches are fitted with glass on the back of the watchcase. Except Rolex, that is. In fact, you can own a Rolex for an entire lifetime and never see the movement. This is a shame. So when you take your watch in for a service, ask if they would mind removing the back of the watchcase just for a moment, so you can see the movement.

The current Rolex movements can be called third generation. Like everything else, the movements are continually improved, but the basic construction hasn't changed. The upside is that the movement in your Rolex offers superior reliability. You can easily find more sophisticated movements than the ones used by Rolex, but they won't be more reliable. Reliability is one of the key selling points when choosing a Rolex. It will easily withstand racing a yacht, playing golf, a game of tennis or a swim in the Red Sea.

There are quite a few fine watches on the market, for which physical activities will result in a service bill from the local watchmaker that might easily amount to more than you paid to play golf in the first place.

Today, Rolex exclusively use self-winding movements, the so-called automatic. Every time you move your wrist, the movement stores the energy in a spring, just as it would if you were winding the watch. You can still wind the watch manually, and this is typically done when you won't be wearing the watch for a few days – or if it's been left for a longer period of time, and the energy stored in the spring has been used up. The energy is collected by a half-moon-shaped oscillating rotor that always moves in the same direction. The collected energy is then stored in the so-called 'Blue Parachrome Hairspring'. Another term you will come across when reading the specifications for a watch movement, is the number of jewels. They are used to reduce the friction between the moving parts. Most Rolex movements use 31 jewels, though the Daytona uses 41 because of the complex chronograph function.

The first self-winding watch movement was developed in 1923 by John Harwood and used in a wristwatch called *The Bumper*. However, Rolex improved Harwood's invention. In *The Bumper*, the rotor only rotated 300 degrees. Rolex improved this to 360 degrees, and because the rotor only needed to travel in one direction, it could collect more energy.

It also gave superior precision, and in 1910, as the first ever wristwatch, Rolex was officially certified by the Contrôle Officiel Suisse des Chronomètres – or just COSC. Even today, every single Rolex is still tested and certified by the COSC. And so far every Rolex ever tested has passed.

The movement in a Rolex is a so-called automatic. When you move your wrist, the movement stores the energy in a spring, just as it would if you wound the watch

THE BOOK OF
ROLEX

A ROLEX NEEDS TIME

Manufacturing a Rolex is a comprehensive process, and before you receive your new watch, rest assured it has been both crash-tested and dropped on the floor

If you own a Rolex, you're probably aware that every step of its production demands exceptional craftsmanship and an unparalleled attention to detail. But how long does it actually take to manufacture your watch?

That's a question that's difficult to answer definitively, as it depends heavily on the specific model. Rolex operate several facilities: their headquarters are in Geneva, movements are made in Bienne, cases and bracelets in Plan-les-Ouates where their foundry is also located, and in Chêne-Bourg they handle bezels and gem setting. No, you cannot visit these facilities no matter how many Rolex watches you own, as Rolex maintain a notoriously closed operation. What we do know is that Rolex produce more than one million watches annually, equating to approximately 3,200 watches per day. Each watch is the result of a complex and lengthy process involving incredible amounts of manual labour from skilled specialists, despite some processes sounding almost comical at times.

Take, for instance, the dial of your Rolex, which has literally been intentionally dropped on the floor to ensure that the indices and markers, meticulously placed by a skilled watchmaker, stay securely in place.

As mentioned, Rolex are a closed enterprise that rarely disclose details about their manufacturing processes. From their own advertisements over the years, we know that it takes three hours and 30 minutes to assemble a Rolex watch. However, this is just one step in a long process. Before assembly, Rolex must manufacture the many components required. For example, crafting the ceramic Cerachrom bezel takes approximately 40 hours.

Once assembled, each watch undergoes rigorous testing to ensure it meets Rolex's exacting standards, both internally and at COSC (Contrôle Officiel Suisse des Chronomètres). This testing primarily ensures that the watch is waterproof. Divers' watches are subjected to 25 per cent more pressure than they are rated to withstand. Thus, every Rolex Deepsea undergoes testing at 4.5 tons of pressure, equivalent to the pressure at a depth of 3,900 metres – plus an additional 25 per cent.

The toughest test is the impact test, where a Rolex is subjected to a shock of 5,000 g-forces – several hundred times more than what you would experience in a serious car accident. The watch must not only remain undamaged but also fully functional after this test. In total, there are 26 different tests each watch must pass before leaving the factory. Each component is handcrafted before being assembled, adding to the meticulous nature of Rolex's manufacturing process.

As for how long it takes from the start of production until you have your new watch in hand, Rolex's marketing indicates it typically takes about a year.

> The toughest test is the hammer test, where a Rolex is subjected to an impact of 5,000 g-forces. The watch must remain undamaged and also fully functional

THE BOOK OF ROLEX

THE PRESIDENTS' WATCH
DAY-DATE

Martin Luther King wore a Day-Date, just like a number of presidents and world leaders, because even if it's expensive and prestigious, it's also very discreet

Day-Date became known as the **PRESIDENTS' WATCH**. *During the Cold War, everybody knew* **THE RED PHONE**. *And the man with the finger on the button wore a* **DAY-DATE**, *according to Rolex.*

THE BOOK OF
ROLEX

VERY FEW *wristwatches can carry* **MOTHER-OF-PEARL** *like a Day-Date, but in gold, it becomes* **ELEGANT**.

The Day-Date is only produced in **PRECIOUS METALS**, *with options including gold, white gold, platinum, or Rolex's special* **EVEROSE ALLOY**, *as seen here.*

The special **ICE-BLUE COLOUR** *of the dial indicates that it is the* **PLATINUM** *model. The Day-Date was launched in 1956 as the first wristwatch to display both the date and the* **DAY OF THE WEEK**.

The Day-Date is available in **TWO CLASSIC SIZES**: *36 millimetres, reflecting the classic men's watch size of the 1950s, and* **40 MILLIMETRES**, *which is more contemporary.*

The Day-Date is synonymous with **PRECIOUS METALS** *and, on many models, also diamonds. Here in* **36 MILLIMETRES**, *perhaps the most* **BLINGY** *watch from Rolex today!*

THE BOOK OF
ROLEX

Two generations of **ROLEX DAY-DATE**. *On the right, the first one from 1956, on the left, the current model – typical Rolex, not much has changed.*

The Day-Date is only available in gold or platinum and it does come with a hefty price tag, but at the same time it's so discreet that it's often mistaken for the less expensive Datejust. But then, if you wear a Day-Date, chances are you don't need to show off. This is a watch for presidents, the world's most powerful CEOs and world leaders, who wish to have the best Rolex have to offer, but who also value subtlety. Celebrities like Martin Luther King, Sylvester Stallone and President John F. Kennedy have one thing in common: they all wore a Day-Date.

It's the model for the true aficionados. It comes with the best movement that Rolex can offer and the best bracelet. In 1956, when the model was first introduced, it was one of the first watches that could display the date on the watchface. This still applies to the Day-Date, with one important addition. These days you can specify up to 26 different languages.

At midnight, both date and the day of the week change in a split second. To make life easier for those who travel between different parts of the world, the 'Double Quick Set' function was introduced in 1986. This way you can move back and forth between different time zones in just a moment, with no need for the hands to make a full rotation.

All things are relative of course. The Day-Date is also available in a number of versions that show off exactly what this watch is. Both the watch dial and bezel can be decorated with diamonds and precious stones.

Day-Date is only delivered with the President bracelet. This is the finest bracelet that Rolex offer, and it fits around your wrist like an exclusive piece of jewellery. The President bracelet was actually introduced a couple of years before the Day-Date, but the two were bound to meet.

Like every other Rolex, the Day-Date has also been enhanced over the years, and there have been few exceptions to the rule. In 1963 Rolex actually did manufacture a Day-Date in steel, but they only ever made six examples, which were presented to the honour students at the school of watchmakers, École d'horlogerie de Genève. However, don't expect to make much of a saving if you come across one of these rare watches. In 2012 one of the steel Day-Dates came up for auction, and sold for CHf50,600, which is more or less what you will be required to pay for a Day-Date in platinum.

Among Rolex enthusiasts, the model is know as The President, since Kennedy, Nixon and Roosevelt among others, took to wearing a Day-Date when in office. The tradition is believed to have started when Rolex presented Dwight D. Eisenhower with a Day-Date as he took office. Until then, Eisenhower had worn a Datejust.

Day-Date is still available in the classic 36 millimetres. In 2008 Rolex introduced a 41-millimetre version, which has now been replaced by the current 40-millimetre Day-Date. It comes with a new calibre, with an impressive 70 hours' power reserve. With the new version, Rolex also introduced a number of new colours, as well as models with diamonds and other precious stones. So the Day-Date can be either discreet or with bling, but one thing will never change; it will always be known as The President, and if a lady becomes president, Rolex is ready.

> **Celebrities like Martin Luther King, Sylvester Stallone and President Kennedy have one thing in common: they all wore a Rolex Day-Date**

THE BOOK OF
ROLEX

It's a bit hard to picture **PRESIDENT KENNEDY** *with this model, isn't it? Maybe* **MARILYN MONROE**, *but not John F. Kennedy...*

More jewellery than **WATCH**, *perhaps. In the smaller* **36-MILLIMETRE** *version, the model is popular among women.*

The bold **COLOURS** *are among the things that have been introduced to the* **DAY-DATE** *in recent years. When did you last see a watch in this* **HUE**?

90

THE BOOK OF
ROLEX

A Day-Date in gold with the so-called **PRESIDENT BRACELET.** *You can see how it would fit* **PERFECTLY** *around your wrist, can't you?*

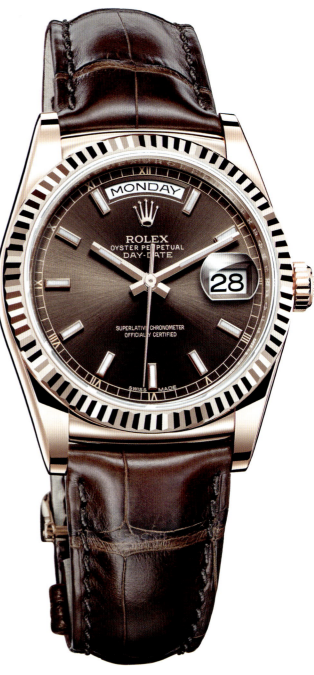

Day-Date in **EVEROSE GOLD** *leaves you in no doubt that this is an exclusive watch. But the* **LEATHER STRAP** *brings it all down a notch to make the combination classic and* **TASTEFUL.**

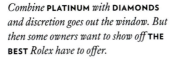

Combine **PLATINUM** *with* **DIAMONDS** *and discretion goes out the window. But then some owners want to show off* **THE BEST** *Rolex have to offer.*

91

THE BOOK OF
ROLEX

WHEN A ROLEX BECOMES
VINTAGE

Rolex's older models have always been popular, but it's worth remembering that when you buy vintage, you're not just buying a watch, you're buying a seller

Remember that Rolex is more than just the **SUBMARINER**, **GMT** *and* **DAYTONA**. *Models like the classic* **EXPLORER** *are often overlooked, making their prices more* **REASONABLE** *as a result.*

ROLEX DAYTONA *in the legendary 1965 edition, featuring the so-called* **PAUL NEWMAN DIAL**. *At the time, it was Rolex's most* **UNPOPULAR** *model, but today, it is the* **MOST SOUGHT AFTER**...

THE BOOK OF
ROLEX

Buying a vintage Rolex can be quite enchanting. Perhaps it's because they hail from a time when the world seemed less complex, or because they boast a special patina and history. They also tend to be smaller and, let's be honest, more discreet and authentic compared to newer models.

However, purchasing a vintage Rolex is more demanding than buying a new one, and the first challenge is determining exactly what you want. There are thousands of different watches out there, ranging from the good and the bad, to the ones you should steer clear of, such as 'Frankenstein' watches and skilful forgeries. Moreover, each model has numerous variations, which can be confusing unless you're well versed in their reference numbers. Thankfully, there are many websites dedicated to helping you navigate these nuances. Seek out those which are passionate about watches and avoid those merely interested in flaunting their knowledge to anyone who will listen. In other words, don't start searching until you're certain of what you're looking for.

And what might that be? That's the big question, of course. It's easy enough to decide on a Daytona or a Submariner, as they have rightfully become timeless classics, but they also come with a hefty price tag.

What about an Oyster Perpetual or an early Air-King? Here, you get a lot of watch for your money, especially when considering models smaller than the now standard 40 millimetres. It wasn't long ago that 36 millimetres was the standard size for a men's watch, and our wrists haven't grown larger since then.

Next, you need to buy the seller, not just the watch. It's more important to purchase a watch from someone you trust than to snag a cheap timepiece that turns out to be worthless. This may sound trivial, but people are often swindled because they finally find the watch of their dreams at an incredible price – actually, a steal! Here are two solid pieces of advice: Never buy a Rolex you haven't held in your hand, nor one that hasn't been inspected by someone knowledgeable in such matters. If the seller seems unsavoury, then they are not the one from whom you should buy a Rolex. Trust your instincts, and if they're not good, be prepared to walk away. In reality, buying from the right seller is more crucial than buying the right watch. Purchasing privately always carries risks, but there are numerous reputable vintage-watch dealers who excel at finding what they don't already have.

Next, consider maintenance. All watches, especially vintage ones, require upkeep and servicing, much like your car. It demands the right tools, special oils, and skilled hands. Naturally, this costs money, but skipping maintenance can cost even more.

If there's no documentation showing that the watch you're interested in has been serviced, remember that people sell things for a reason.

A vintage Rolex is akin to an older house or classic car. It requires that you understand how it operates. But if you buy the right one and take care of it, it will endure long after you're gone.

> You should never buy a Rolex that you haven't held in your hand. Trust your instincts, and if they aren't good, be ready to walk away

CERTIFIED PRE-OWNED *is Rolex's own programme for vintage models that are sold through* **AUTHORISED DEALERS.**

VINTAGE FROM ROLEX

Today, you can buy one of Rolex's vintage models which has been meticulously inspected and certified, from one of their dealers

In recent years, Rolex and many other fine watch manufacturers have experienced a significant surge in demand, and even with a production of over a million watches per year, Rolex are struggling to meet that demand.

This has resulted in customers having to wait several years to get their new watch, creating a whole new market where those who don't want to wait are willing to pay a premium. A new Rolex can usually be sold for a solid profit the moment it's picked up from one of Rolex's dealers.

This has led to increased demand for vintage models and given new momentum to those who produce counterfeits and the so-called Frankenstein watches – clever forgeries made with a mixture of genuine and fake parts to make them harder to distinguish from the real thing.

It's this issue that Rolex have decided to address with their Certified Pre-Owned models, which are older models that have been inspected, serviced and certified by Rolex, with a guarantee of condition and authenticity. This makes it possible to buy a new old watch.

The programme was launched in 2022 in Switzerland, Austria, Germany, France, the UK and Denmark, and allows customers to purchase a pre-owned version of an older model, but one that has been inspected and approved by Rolex, ensuring there is no doubt about its authenticity, guaranteed by one of Rolex's official dealers, many of which are owned by the Swiss factory.

Specifically, the watches included in the programme must be at least three years old at the time they are resold by a Rolex dealer. Before that, they are disassembled and meticulously inspected by Rolex and their experts to ensure everything is correct, and all parts are original and match the reference number.

If the watch passes this inspection, it is approved as Certified Pre-Owned. It is then serviced, any parts that don't meet Rolex standards are replaced and, finally, it is polished to appear like new before being offered for sale.

When you purchase a Certified Pre-Owned Rolex, you have the assurance that you are buying a vintage watch in the best possible condition, with even the smallest details as they should be, having been inspected by the experts who know these watches best. There's also no doubt that these watches will be in demand.

The programme aims to facilitate a larger share of vintage-model sales through Rolex's official dealers, recognising that the older models often last more than one lifetime.

Additionally, it is, of course, about the rising prices increasing interest among those who produce the many counterfeits out there, and unfortunately, they are constantly improving.

> For Rolex, it's about the sale of vintage models through authorised dealers, because those who make counterfeit watches are constantly improving

If you don't have the budget for a **RED SUB** *with* **BOX AND PAPERS**, *you can find one without. But buy from a seller* **WITH A GOOD REPUTATION**.

THE BOOK OF

ROLEX

THE HUNT FOR A RED SUB

While in California, Jens Høy became captivated by the desire for a vintage Red Sub with neither box nor papers, but from a dealer with a good reputation...

There comes a time when you just have to have a classic vintage Rolex, and a Submariner with red text – a Red Sub – is the watch many dream of owning. One of these, with the box and all the correct papers, costs a fortune, so another way to go about it is to buy from a reliable dealer, such as Fourtané in Carmel, California.

The store has been owned by the same family since 1950, and anyone who knows a bit about vintage Rolex watches will sooner or later come across John or Joshua Bonifas, who run the shop. They are laid-back in that typical American way, and you can try on everything. Jens quickly found a Submariner Ref. 1680 with the red text on the dial – a 'Red Sub' – for $12,000 (£9,250).

Included was a so-called appraisal, which is a document that describes the watch as accurately as possible. In reality, you are buying a watch you know nothing about, so the dealer's reputation is your only assurance, but it's better than buying the watch from a private seller online, of course.

Still, there's reason to be nervous the day you ask an authorised Rolex dealer to take a closer look at your new watch. Every year, they encounter customers who come into the shop with what they believe to be a genuine Rolex, only to discover that they have bought a watch that isn't what it claims to be.

It could be that the movement isn't original or that the watch has been repaired with non-genuine parts. Today, Rolex have tightened the rules on what their authorised dealers are allowed to do, and if there's anything in your watch that isn't as it should be, you won't be able to get it serviced at an authorised dealer.

If you plan to keep the watch and pass it down as an heirloom, it doesn't matter if you have to take it to a regular watchmaker for servicing. But if you intend to sell the watch, buying something that's not completely genuine could become costly, and if a major problem arises, Rolex won't be able to help you.

The issues became apparent as soon as the watchmaker unscrewed the caseback. The watch had probably suffered a heavy blow, which is why there were metal shavings in the thread when the case was opened.

Fortunately, the thread wasn't damaged to the point where the case couldn't be closed again, and the back of the case had '3rd month of 1969' stamped on it, which confirmed the appraisal that came with the watch.

After a thorough examination, the watchmaker concluded that there was some corrosion in the mid-case, but that this was entirely normal for a watch of its age. The case itself was slightly deformed, but not enough to affect the water resistance of the watch.

All in all, the authorised Rolex dealer judged the watch to be in excellent condition. The dial and bezel were perfect; the hands had been exposed to a bit of moisture, but the overall condition was really good with a perfect patina, and the movement was found to be in excellent condition.

Lastly, the watch was pressure tested, and a two-year warranty on the repair was issued. This essentially serves as a certificate of authenticity; if anything non-genuine had been found during the process, the watch would have been rejected immediately.

For this reason, if you're going to buy a vintage Rolex without a box or papers, make sure you do so from a dealer you trust.

> Today, Rolex have tightened the rules, so if there is anything in your watch that isn't as it should be, you cannot get it serviced at an authorised dealer

UP CLOSE *you can enjoy the watch bezel in Cerachrom. The ceramic material is the result of Rolex's constant research into* **NEW MATERIALS**, *it's almost impossible to scratch and even more difficult* **TO FAKE.**

THE BOOK OF
ROLEX

THE PILOT'S WATCH
GMT-MASTER

Many years ago the American airline Pan-Am asked Rolex if it would be possible to make a watch with dual time zones. The result became the GMT-Master

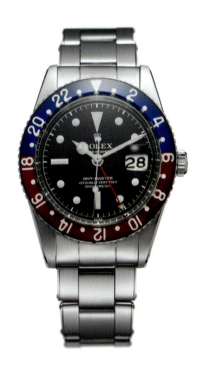

The first **GMT-MASTER** *with the characteristic 'Pepsi' bezel in red and blue, which makes it possible to see* **TWO TIME ZONES** *simultaneously.*

THE BOOK OF
ROLEX

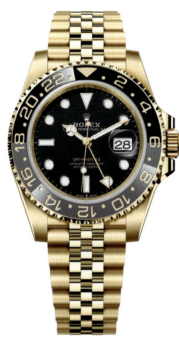

The first **GOLD VERSION** *was introduced in the 1970s, when buyers demanded a bit more bling on the model made famous by the pilots from the* **US AIR FORCE** *and guerrilla leaders like* **CHE GUEVARA** *and* **FIDEL CASTRO**.

The new **GMT-MASTER II** *with the classic* **PEPSI** *bezel. The colour is shot into the ceramic material in a very* **ADVANCED PROCESS**.

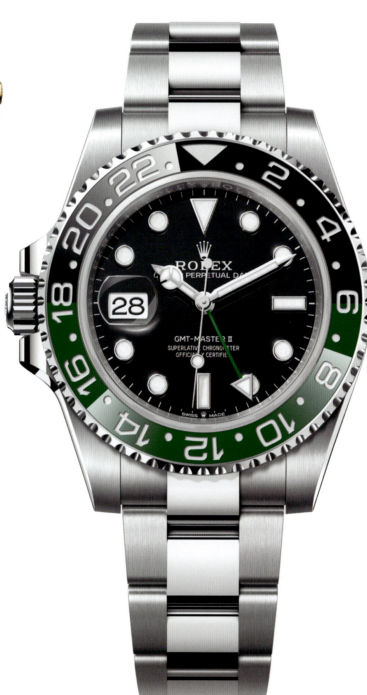

Look at the crown, placed on the **OPPOSITE SIDE** *of where you normally find it. This GMT-Master is made for* **LEFT-HANDED** *Rolex owners. Like a lot of other things, watches are usually designed for* **RIGHT-HANDED** *people.*

If the bezel is **RED AND BLUE**, *it's a 'Pepsi' – here in the version with a dial made from a meteorite from* **OUTER SPACE**.

The bezel leads to the **NICKNAME**. *If it's black and brown like this one, it's called a* **ROOT BEER** *because of the resemblance to the label of the* **AMERICAN SOFT DRINK**.

THE BOOK OF
ROLEX

Anyone can wear a **GMT-MASTER**. **LUCA DI MONTEZEMOLO**, *the former boss of* **FERRARI**, *photographed at the Italian Grand Prix at Monza, guerrilla leader* **CHE GUEVARA**, *and the dream of many women in the 1980s, actor* **TOM SELLECK**, *playing his defining role as* **MAGNUM P.I**.

Things happened quickly in 1954. A new generation of passenger planes with jet-engines made it possible to fly across oceans and continents and the buzz word in the airline industry was 'non-stop'. However, this presented the pilots with a new challenge, because they needed to keep track of several time zones when navigating and receiving weather updates. The longer flights also gave birth to a new word: 'jetlag'.

American airline Pan-Am was among the first to fly the transatlantic routes non-stop, and to solve the problem of telling the time they approached Rolex, by then famous for their professional diving watches. If Rolex could make a watch that could display two time zones, then Pan-Am would like to buy one for each and every one of their pilots.

Rolex quickly saw the potential for the project. A watch like that wouldn't just be popular with the pilots from Pan-Am, but with pilots everywhere – not to mention anyone who dreamed of becoming a pilot. Airline pilots were the heroes of the day, since they would freight the so-called jet set (another new word) around the world. The new model did indeed become an instant success, and it didn't hurt that both NASA and the US Air Force quickly made the Rolex GMT-Master part of their pilots' standard issue.

The solution to displaying the dual time zones was an extra hand that took 24 hours to complete a rotation. By having a 24-hour indication on the watch bezel, the pilots were able to see both the time zone they were coming from as well as the one they were going to, or the so-called Greenwich Mean Time (GMT) that gave the model its name. This used to be the time zone in which all flight plans and weather reports were issued, though it was replaced by CUT – Coordinated Universal Time – in 1972. This eliminated mistakes and made it easier for the pilots to navigate when flying through several time zones. The GMT-Master also became popular among passengers, because if you know the time at the place you departed from, it has a positive influence on jetlag.

The first GMT-Master was the Ref. 6242 which was introduced in 1954 with a watch bezel in Bakelite. This was quickly replaced by a bezel in aluminium, since Bakelite would crack quite easily. One of the most popular vintage models is the Ref. 1675 GMT-Master produced from 1959 to 1980, which makes this one of the most enduring Rolex models.

The GMT-Master II was introduced in the early 1980s. They look identical, and the original GMT-Master continued in production until the end of the 1990s, but there are important differences between the two. Most important was a function in the movement enabling the large hand to jump at a pre-set interval without stopping the seconds hand or the GMT-hand. This way it was possible to display a third time zone.

The original GMT-Master was a so-called tool watch, and as such only available in steel until the 1970s, when the first versions in gold were introduced. In 2005 Rolex updated the model with a new design, first of all a new and wider watch bezel in the new ceramic material Cerachrom. Initially only available in black, the classic combination of blue and red quickly followed, though by then Pan-Am had gone out of business.

> A new generation of passenger planes with jet-engines made it possible to cross oceans and continents, and the buzz word of the day was 'non-stop'

The Rolex GMT-Master II displays **MULTIPLE TIME ZONES** *with precision. The 24-hour hand works in conjunction with the bidirectional rotatable bezel, allowing you to easily track a* **SECOND TIME ZONE** *or synchronise with a third by adjusting the bezel.*

In 2017, the **SKY-DWELLER** *came in this version, which combines Rolex's distinctive* **YELLOW ROLESOR** *with steel, an elegant combination.*

THE BOOK OF
ROLEX

THE BUSINESSMAN'S WATCH
SKY-DWELLER

When the Sky-Dweller was introduced in 2012, it wasn't just a new model, but the first Rolex with a complication, something the iconic brand had never offered before

The **HEART** *of the Sky-Dweller is the* **CALIBRE 9002**, *which keeps track of the* **DATE**, *the* **MONTH** *and, of course,* **TWO TIME ZONES**.

THE BOOK OF ROLEX

The **SKY-DWELLER** *is one of Rolex's larger models at* **42 MILLIMETRES** *and is available with the special* **OYSTERFLEX BRACELET**, *which has a titanium core.*

GOLD *on the bracelet, case and dial. In this edition the Sky-Dweller becomes a real* **GENTLEMAN'S WATCH**, *if you can afford it.*

It's almost become sporty! But the **SKY-DWELLER** *is also available in this version in* **WHITE ROLESOR** *and steel, with the distinctive* **GREEN DIAL**.

Like the **DAY-DATE**, *the Sky-Dweller is only available in* **PRECIOUS METAL**. *In white gold, as seen here, it's almost* **UNDERSTATED**.

Here in **EVEROSE GOLD**. *Previously, the Sky-Dweller was available with* **ROMAN NUMERALS**, *but those models have now been* **DISCONTINUED**.

THE BOOK OF ROLEX

Rotating the **WATCH BEZEL** *adjusts the annual calendar and both the time zones, and because of the way the bezel is designed, you can't tell it's been* **ADJUSTED**.

The rectangular **RED INDICATOR** *shows the month. However, since this is a mechanical watch, the annual calendar has to be set in* **FEBRUARY** *every year.*

THE DATE *is shown through a Cyclops lens and follows the* **LOCAL TIME ZONE**. *It automatically skips a day in months with* **JUST 30 DAYS**.

The central **SUBDIAL** *shows the second time zone, and of course this is done in* **24 HOURS**, *so you know if it's* **DAY OR NIGHT** *back home.*

The thing everyone was waiting for at Baselworld 2012 was the new model from Rolex. The first rumours appeared when it became known that Rolex had registered the name 'Sky-Dweller'. It's not every day that the iconic Swiss manufacturer introduces a brand new model series. In fact, it's not even every decade.

The expectation was that it would be a sports model, and probably a more luxurious version of the GMT-Master, in the same way that the Sea-Dweller is a more luxurious version of the Submariner, but Rolex surprised everybody. The Sky-Dweller was something completely new from Rolex, and for a whole new audience. It has two time zones displayed in a new way, as well as an annual calendar, displaying not just the month but also the date. Oh, and it certainly isn't a sports watch. The best way to describe the Sky-Dweller is as a dress watch you can wear every day, and with a 42-millimetre watchcase it's one of the largest models offered by Rolex. If anything, it's related to the Day-Date, since neither of these two models is available in steel. To date, the Sky-Dweller only comes in gold.

Below the crown on the watchface is a red arrow pointing to the 24-hour scale on the subdial. This displays the second time zone which can be adjusted independently of the first. When it comes to displaying two time zones on a mechanical watch, it doesn't come any easier, and ease of use is the point of the Sky-Dweller. With the time zones displayed like this you always know what time it is back home. The watch hands show the local time, and they determine the annual calendar which changes in a split-second at midnight.

The calendar is interesting since it also displays the month. With watches this is what's known as a complication. Some watch manufacturers can't get enough of these, but Rolex had always avoided them. Until now, that is. The way it's engineered is a stroke of genius, since it only required four extra gears to be added to the existing calendar function to create the annual calendar. However, since this is still a mechanical watch, it needs to be set manually every year at the end of February.

Rolex have named the invention SAROS, from the Greek word for the 18-year cycle between the Earth, Sun and Moon, which also dictates the solar and lunar eclipses. The annual calendar is built around a planetary gear, which gives an extra pulse in April, June, September and November – the four months of the year just 30 days long. Here the date changes twice. The month itself is shown by the small red indicator on the edge of the watchface.

Just as with the dual time zones, rotating the bezel controls the calendar. It's simple and intuitive to use, but a very complex piece of engineering. It consists of 60 individual components and makes the Sky-Dweller unique. Because of the so-called fluted design, you can't see it's been rotated.

Another addition is the new movement called Calibre 9001, which is the most complicated movement ever manufactured by Rolex. It beats 28,800 times per hour, and even with the SAROS system it still retains a 72-hour power reserve in this big, complicated and elegant watch.

Until now Rolex had avoided complications, but not any longer. However, the true genius is in how easy it is to set and read the annual calendar and time zones.

> Until now Rolex had avoided complications, but not any longer. However, the true genius is in how easy it is to set and read the annual calendar and time zones

*Rolex's first **complication** is seen here up close. On the dial in the centre, you have the **additional time zone**, and within the bezel, the annual calendar with the **12 months**.*

THE BOOK OF
ROLEX

THE FAKE
ROLEX

Rolex is not just one of the most popular Swiss watches, it's also the favourite among those who make fake watches, so be very careful when purchasing online

THE BOOK OF
ROLEX

A genuine **ROLEX GMT-MASTER II** *and a fake, that's relatively easy to spot when you look at the* **CYCLOPS LENS** *which doesn't* **ENLARGE** *the date on the cheap copy. But the best forgeries can be almost* **INDISTINGUISHABLE** *from the real thing.*

THE BOOK OF
ROLEX

A genuine **ROLEX DAYTONA** *costs well over* **£12,000 ($15,000)**, *so making a forgery must be tempting. This model in* **WHITE GOLD** *would be double that price, if it was real, that is. Details like the seconds hand give it away, but* **NOT MANY KNOW THAT.**

ROLEX MILGAUSS *is another favourite with producers of fake watches. The design is simple with the* **CLEAN WATCHCASE** *and solid bezel. This is one of the more expensive fakes which typically costs around* **£600 ($800)**. *Because you so rarely see a Milgauss, it's easy to be fooled by a copy like this.*

THE BOOK OF
ROLEX

The fake **GMT-MASTER II** *from before is easily spotted because of the* **CYCLOPS LENS** *which doesn't enlarge. On the more expensive fakes it will enlarge the date, but typically just 1.5 times – a genuine Cyclops enlarges* **2.5 TIMES**.

T he Rolex you buy on the beach promenade in Pattaya is bound to be a fake, and won't fool anybody. But these are the cheap knock-offs. It gets trickier when you see a Rolex with the right documents and the right box, which were made specifically to fool you.

The best are so accurate that even the professionals from time to time can't say what's what. This is because the people making the fakes are getting more advanced. They will be created using CAD/CAM software, fake documents of authenticity, and even a copy of a Rolex movement. The best fakes can be so accurate that Rolex dealers sometimes send the watches to the factory in Switzerland, for them to determine if the watch is genuine.

The cheapest copies give the game away by using cheap materials, but the best fakes don't do that, and often people don't know they've been cheated until it's too late. Rolex do all they can to stay ahead of the game, such as engraving 'Rolex' between the glass and the watchface, and other small details to make life more difficult for the fakers. Rolex also develop advanced materials like Cerachrom, which is impossible to duplicate. This is why the people making fake watches are now turning their attention to the vintage models, so, as a buyer, you have to pay more attention than ever.

One of the **CHEAPER FAKES**, *easy to spot just on the bezel, which doesn't have the same colour as the* **WATCHFACE**. *This Submariner will only fool those who have never seen a* **REAL ROLEX**.

THE BOOK OF
ROLEX

*This is what Rolex fans call a '**FRANKENSTEIN**'. The Air-King looks every bit a Rolex, and the watchcase, dial and bracelet are genuine. But the movement is an **AUTOMATIC**, which is not found in this model. That means this watch is composed of **GENUINE AND FAKE PARTS**, to make it more difficult to discover that it is not a **ROLEX**.*

FRANKENSTEIN

The best fakes are know as 'Frankenstein watches', since they are a mix of fake and genuine parts, to make you believe you have a real Rolex in your hands

The dial, the hands and the bezel are from a real Rolex, but the watchcase and movement are fake. This is the kind of nightmare you have on your hands when you come across a 'Frankenstein'. Even if you know your Rolex watches, it can fool you, and most who are unfortunate enough to buy these watches, don't realise anything is wrong until they take the watch in for a service. By then the seller will be long gone, and so will the money you paid for the watch.

For the people making 'Frankenstein watches' the idea is simple. You buy a genuine Rolex, and by mixing it with fake parts, turn it into two, three or four watches, which can each be sold as if they were genuine. This is what has happened to the Air-King on the opposite page. By doing it this way, even the skilled buyer can be fooled, and professional watchmakers will have a hard time knowing if the watch is genuine or not.

Another problem is that the fake parts are getting better. These days it's possible to replicate an entire Rolex movement, to a point where it's almost impossible to tell the real and the fake apart. This type of fake used to be quite rare, but not any more. In fact, the forgeries are so accurate these days that even the authorised Rolex dealers won't issue a certificate of authenticity without sending the watch in question to the factory in Switzerland.

Rolex are perfectly willing to determine if your watch is the genuine article. However, before your

> It's worth remembering that the photographs you see online might be of a genuine Rolex, but the watch you receive will be a high-quality forgery

watch can be sent to the factory for evalution, you have to sign a waiver allowing Rolex to destroy your watch if it turns out it's not a genuine Rolex. Even if they don't, they will sand off the Rolex logo on the fake parts. They do this all the time, and even if you go to one of Rolex's authorised dealers, the people who handle vintage watches every day will sometimes be unsure, and then the only way to be sure is to send the watch to the factory.

If you have been unfortunate enough to buy a 'Frankenstein', the situation is hopeless. Most people don't realise they've been cheated until they take the watch in for a service, which can be years after it was purchased. Despite what might be a genuine box from Rolex, all the right paperwork and the genuine part, the watch you bought is now worthless.

Fake watches come in different qualities. The best fakes sold on the internet typically cost up to £450 ($560). It's parts from watches like these that are used to produce a 'Frankenstein', and the result can be very convincing, especially when the buyer only sees the pictures in the ad for an online auction. But it's worth remembering that the photographs might be of a genuine watch, whilst the watch you will receive, will be a high-quality forgery. The buyer won't realise this until it's too late, since the watch will arrive with what appears to be a genuine box and all the right paperwork. All this will be no more genuine than the watch, because making fake Rolex watches is big business.

*A **COSMOGRAPH DAYTONA** in a box from Rolex, but just like the watch, the box is **A FAKE**. Be aware that these things are also made as copies of the real thing, or you can find a fake watch in a **GENUINE BOX** from Rolex.*

THE BOOK OF
ROLEX

THIS COMES WITH A GENUINE ROLEX

CERTIFICATE OF AUTHENTICITY
The documents that show this is a genuine Rolex, the reference serial number of the watch and when it was sold for the first time.

CHRONOMETER CERTIFICATION
This documents that the watch has been approved at the Official Swiss Chronometer Testing Institute (COSC). Keep this with your watch.

INSTRUCTION
An introduction to the functions of the specific model, what movement is used, and so on. Well worth a read, so you'll know your watch.

BROCHURE
The brochure is about your model and other models in the same series. It also gives you a list of dealers and service points around the world.

BITS OF PLASTIC
When you take out your new Rolex, these will attach to the bracelet. Collectors love these so don't throw them away!

GUARANTEE
All new watches from Rolex come with a two-year warranty and can be serviced anywhere in the world. The terms are explained in this little booklet.

FAKE AND GENUINE
The fake Rolex box is on the left, and easy to recognise, because the spacing between the words 'Rolex' and 'Oyster' is wrong. But a fake Rolex can arrive in a genuine box.

Acertificate of authenticity is no guarantee that the watch you're holding is genuine. These items also come as fakes, just like receipts and user manuals.

When you buy a genuine Rolex, it's important to always keep every part that comes with it, including the links you might take out of the bracelet. The same applies to the receipts issued when the watch is serviced. A new Rolex comes with lots of boxes, papers, a user manual, chronometer certifications and little bits and pieces with the Rolex logo. You should keep it all, because these things will become very important should you wish to sell the watch one day. The watch also comes with a transparent film to protect the bracelet and watchcase. Some people leave this on the watch if it's purchased as an investment.

THE BOOK OF ROLEX

This **GMT-MASTER** *has all the right details, like the engravings on the bracelet, but it's a fake. Look for the* **RECEIPT** *from when the watch was serviced, and if it's there, call the* **ROLEX DEALER**.

HOW TO SPOT A FAKE ROLEX

THE DATE
The small bubble over the date is called a Cyclops lens. On a genuine Rolex it enlarges by a factor of 2.5, on a fake watch it enlarges by 1.5 or not at all.

THE SOUND
If you can hear the watch ticking, without holding it to your ear, it's a fake. A Rolex movement gives a very low, but unmistakably very fast, ticking noise.

THE GLASS
With the exception of older vintage models, Rolex watches use sapphire glass. Dip your finger in water, slide it across the glass and if it's sapphire, the water will retract.

THE SECONDS HAND
One misconception about a Rolex is that the seconds hand moves continuously. Take a good look: on a genuine Rolex, the seconds hand makes eight small clicks per second.

THE WRITING ON THE DIAL
Use a magnifying glass. The writing on the dial on a genuine Rolex is perfect. If there's even the slightest error, it's a sure sign the watch is a fake.

THE CROWN
All Rolex watches, apart from some of the earliest examples, have a screw-down crown. Turn it, and if it's a forgery, you can feel the cheaper movement.

THE RECEIPTS
If the watch is more than five years old, a Rolex dealer will have serviced it. That means there's a receipt with a number on it. Call the dealer to make sure the receipt is genuine. If that's the case, then there's a good chance the watch is genuine too. But remember: a fake watch can come with a genuine receipt!

THE HANDS
On a real Rolex, every model has its own characteristic hands. Forgers often use more or less the same hands on every model, so go to the Rolex website and compare.

HOLD IT IN YOUR HAND
Never buy a Rolex you haven't held in your hand. The pictures in the advert might be very convincing, but they might not be of the watch you will receive from the seller.

THE BOOK OF
ROLEX

The sticker on the back has a **3-D EFFECT**, *which was something Rolex did to stop the* **FAKES**. *But on a genuine Rolex this sticker would have* **WORN OFF**.

On the **SPORTS MODELS** *you can turn the bezel. Once you've experienced the unique feeling of turning a* **REAL ROLEX**, *you will know when you're turning the bezel on a fake, unless the watch is a* '**FRANKENSTEIN**' *with a genuine Rolex bezel.*

123

The original **ROLEX MILGAUSS** *was discontinued in 1988, but it returned in* **2007** *in highly polished steel and was completely discontinued in* **2024**.

THE SCIENCE WATCH

MILGAUSS

To produce a wristwatch that could resist a magnetic field of 1,000 gauss, was a gigantic achievement, but the first Milgauss never became a popular model

The first **ROLEX MILGAUSS** *looked slightly like the* **SUBMARINER** *with its rotating bezel, but scientists just aren't as cool as* **DEEP-SEA DIVERS**.

THE BOOK OF ROLEX

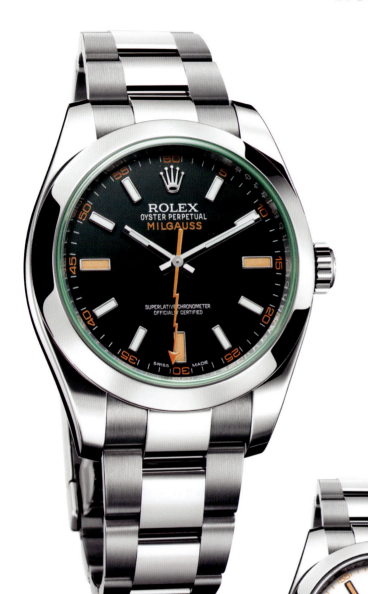

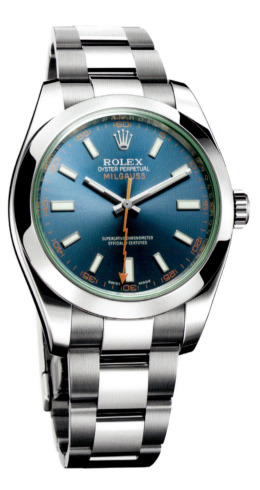

*Orange seconds hand and a dial in **ELECTRIC BLUE**? Rolex is usually quite conservative, but the Milgauss has its own rules and **UNIQUE ELEGANCE**.*

*Milgauss in one of two available **GRAND VERDE** models with the green sapphire glass. It was believed to be a **LIMITED EDITION**, but it's still in production.*

*The standard **MILGAUSS** has a white watchface with **ORANGE** hour markings, clear glass and the trademark seconds hand shaped like a **LIGHTNING BOLT**.*

THE BOOK OF ROLEX

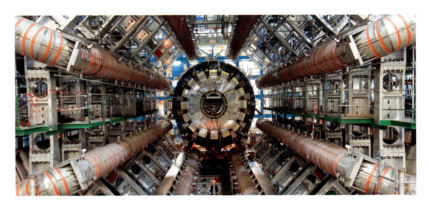

If your **WATCH** *stops displaying time correctly when you are here it's because you don't have a* **MILGAUSS**. *When* **CERN** *tested the watch they concluded it was able to resist magnetic fields up to* **1,000 GAUSS**.

Rolex have always made 'tool watches', which are watches that double as a tool, and have a very specific function. These watches are capable of doing things very few owners will ever subject them to. But we own them because we admire what they can do, or because of a fascination with the technological achievement they represent. After all, very few buy a Rolex Explorer because they intend to climb Mount Everest, and no Rolex Deepsea owner will ever dive to a depth of 13,000 metres.

Nevertheless, the need for specific functions gave us iconic models like the GMT-Master, the Submariner and the Explorer. The same is true for the Milgauss, which quite possibly represents Rolex's greatest achievement. Just as the GMT-Master helped the airline pilots of Pan-Am, the Milgauss was born out of a need to help scientists and other professionals who were faced with a serious problem.

When the strength of a magnetic field reached between 50 and 100 gauss, wristwatches would start acting up, and would no longer display time correctly. This left two options: wear a watch that most likely would never function correctly again, or don't wear a watch at all, when approaching the magnetic field. That last solution would be the choice of someone who has never achieved anything. If you adopt the scientific approach, on the other hand, this is a delightful problem that needs a solution.

The solution was the Rolex Milgauss. The first generation was introduced back in the 1950s. The watch was tested by CERN, the European organisation for particle physics, who later constructed the world-famous particle accelerator at Geneva in Switzerland, where the Milgauss supposedly is in style. CERN concluded that the Milgauss is capable of withstanding magnetic fields up to 1,000 gauss.

The name comes from the Latin word for 'thousand' – *mille* – and gauss, the unit used to measure magnetic fields. Unlike models such as the GMT-Master, the Submariner and Explorer, the first Milgauss never became a popular model. Scientists, it would seem, didn't have the same appeal as airline pilots, deep-sea divers or mountain climbers.

Despite the first Milgauss from 1956 having a design inspired by the Submariner, it never sold very well and disappeared from the line-up in 1988. You would think this would be the end of the Milgauss, but in 2007 the model returned in a brand new design with three different versions, all fitted with the characteristic orange seconds hand shaped like a lightning bolt.

The watchcase itself is thicker than the Submariner's, but still waterproof to a depth of 100 metres. It comes with three different colours for the dial. The standard version can be white or electric blue, and then there is the so-called Grand Verde version with the green-tinted sapphire glass. When it came out, it was believed the GV-version was a limited edition, but it's still in production.

The new Milgauss has a shield around the Calibre 3131 in a unique aluminium alloy, engraved with a 'B' and an arrow, the symbol for magnetic flux density. Few know what this means, but in all likelihood, only your authorised Rolex dealer will ever see it.

> When the strength of a magnetic field reached 50–100 gauss, watches would start acting up. In other words, the scientists of this world had a problem

127

*The green **SAPPHIRE GLASS** has a unique look. Milgauss is the only model from **ROLEX** that uses tinted glass, and even then it's only used for the **GRAND VERDE VERSION**.*

*The Submariner is still available **WITHOUT DATE**, giving a cleaner and more symmetrical dial, a design that also harks back to the original Submariner from 1953, before the **CYCLOPS LENS** was invented.*

THE BOOK OF
ROLEX

THE WORKHORSE
SUBMARINER

When the first Submariner was introduced in 1954, it set new standards for diving watches, and quickly became an essential accessory for the well-dressed gentleman

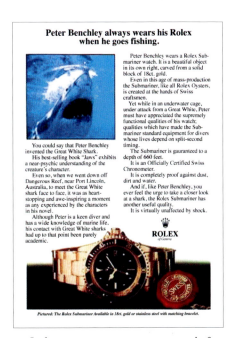

In the 1970s **PETER BENCHLEY** *was enough of a celebrity to be in a testimonial for the* **ROLEX SUBMARINER**. *It was Benchley who wrote the script for the Hollywood movie* **JAWS**.

THE BOOK OF
ROLEX

*The bezel on the Submariner has become **WIDER** over the years, and today it is made of **CERACHROM**, which is virtually **IMPOSSIBLE** to scratch!*

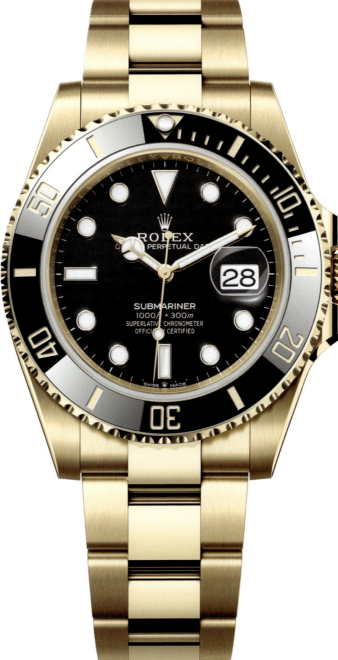

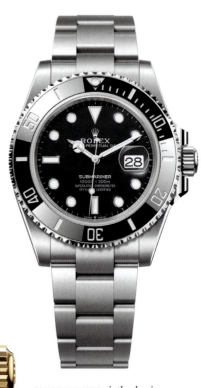

BLACK AND STEEL *is the classic Submariner, and Rolex will **ALWAYS** keep it in the line-up for those who are not into **GOLD AND COLOURS**.*

*1953 was the year the first **SUBMARINER** was introduced, as the first **DIVE WATCH** that was waterproof down to 100 **METRES**.*

*When the **SUBMARINER** was introduced, it was only available in **STEEL**. That has changed since, and today the model is, of course, also available in **GOLD**!*

*When your Submariner has a blue dial and bezel it's a **BLUESY**. Needless to say, blue is a popular colour for the Submariner, which was developed for **DIVING** and underwater adventures.*

THE BOOK OF
ROLEX

The fluorescent markings are useful at **60 METRES' DEPTH**, *but what made the Submariner so successful was when it became* **FASHIONABLE**. *James Bond wore it, as* **ROGER MOORE** *does here, as did other celebrities. And doesn't* **JACQUES COUSTEAU** *send a slightly envious look towards his son's* **SUBMARINER**?

Hans Wilsdorf was more than just a skilled businessman with a great talent for marketing his products. Throughout his career he kept an open mind and listened to the people around him. When René-Paul Jeanneret wasn't working for Rolex he was a passionate diver, and the one who had the idea of a diving watch, one which was elegant and compact enough that you could wear it every day.

At the time Rolex was already quite successful with the Oyster series, which was both sporty and waterproof, but it still wasn't quite what Jeanneret had in mind. Rolex started producing diving watches in the 1930s. If you look in the catalogue from 1935, you will see a model with the reference number 2533, featuring a square watchcase and a diameter of 47 millimetres. However, that model paved the way for a closer collaboration with Panerai, Rolex's main dealer in Italy at the time and an expert in diving equipment. The first watches from Panerai used the same almost-square watchcases, and Rolex apparently learned a lot about diving watches from this project.

The Submariner also marked the beginning of the so-called 'tool watch' — a watch designed for a specific environment, or to do a certain job, like the Explorer, Milgauss or GMT-Master. Wilsdorf quickly learned how well these models would sell, by being both functional and fashionable at the same time, something that still holds true today. A Submariner quickly became an essential accessory for any man, but a Rolex was never only about style. When required, it will do just what it says on the watchface.

The first Submariner was presented in 1954 at the annual watch fair in Basel. That year the big news from Rolex was a professional diving watch that would handle depths of up to 100 metres thanks to the new screw-down crown called the Twinlock. As always, the new model had been thoroughly tested before it was launched, and the results were verified by the prestigious Deep Sea Research Institute in Cannes, who performed no less than 132 dives in the Mediterranean.

In fact, the institute in Cannes had never tried a diving watch which performed as flawlessly as the new Submariner. At the time, every other diving watch they had tested, all showed signs of moisture inside the watchcase, as soon as they were submerged in water, where a slight condensation was visible on the inside of the glass. The Submariner didn't do this, not even when the institute's divers unscrewed the crown to the position used to set the watch, and then took it down to 60 metres, the maximum depth achievable with modern diving equipment. Finally, the Submariner was tied to a line and lowered to 120 metres' depth for an hour. When it returned to the surface, there was no sign of moisture, and despite the massive pressure, it was still working perfectly.

When developing the Submariner, Rolex made good use of input from professional divers and René-Paul Jeanneret, who came up with the idea of the rotating bezel, which shows the diver how much diving time is left. Sixty years ago this was a revolution that has since been copied by many other watchmakers making diving watches.

The same can be said about the Submariner. Since it was introduced, it has defined the look of the modern diving watch.

> The experts from the Deep Sea Research Institute in Cannes sent the new Rolex to a depth of 120 metres, twice what's possible with modern diving equipment

THE BOOK OF
ROLEX

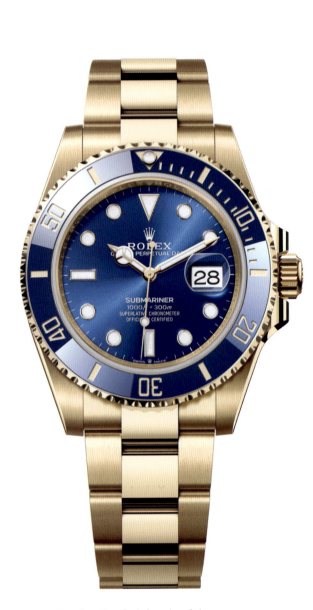

For a long time the Submariner, being a **TOOL WATCH**, *was only available in steel, but these days even the classic 'Sub' comes in* **GOLD**.

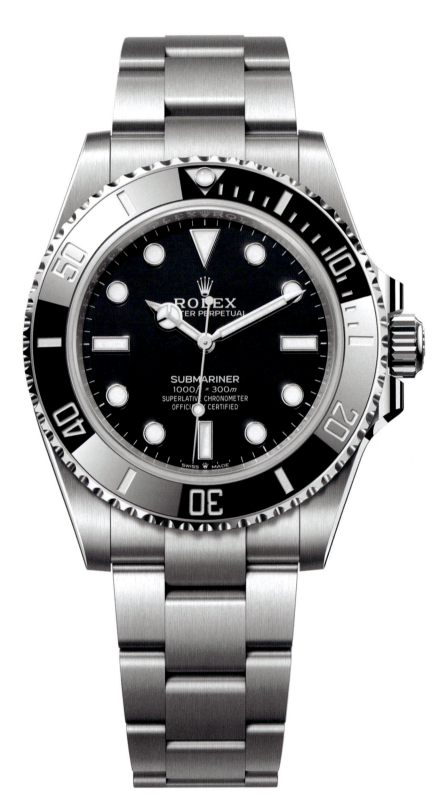

Note the **ABSENCE OF THE DATE**. *It wasn't until* **1969** *that Rolex introduced the* **SUBMARINER WITH A DATE**, *and today you can still choose the model without it, as shown here.*

THE BOOK OF
ROLEX

TWO GENERATIONS of the Submariner **KERMIT MODEL**, which celebrated its **50TH ANNIVERSARY** in 2004. On the newer one at the bottom, you can see how much the watch bezel has **GROWN**.

The first **SUBMARINER** *from 1954. It's different from the current model, but even though it's more than* **60 YEARS OLD**, *the classic Rolex design is instantly* **RECOGNISABLE**.

*Three generations of the **ROLEX SUBMARINER**. The name itself was only added at the end of **1954**, and the early models didn't have the date or the **CROWN GUARDS**.*

THE BOOK OF
ROLEX

KNOW YOUR ROLEX'S
NICKNAME

When talking about Rolex watches, you need to be able to tell the Paul Newman
and the Kermit, from the Hulk, the McQueen and the James Bond

THE BOOK OF ROLEX

#1 BATMAN
The GMT-MASTER, when it has the blue and black bezel, like BATMAN'S mask.

#2 CREAM
Used for both the EXPLORER and the DAYTONA with the CREAM-COLOURED watchface.

#3 BART SIMPSON
Refers to older SUBMARINERS, where the Rolex crown on the dial is printed, so it looks a bit like BART SIMPSON'S hair!

#4 BIG RED
DAYTONA REF. 6263 where 'Daytona' is printed on the dial in RED LETTERS.

#5 COKE
The GMT-MASTER with the bezel in black and red like the classic COCA-COLA bottle.

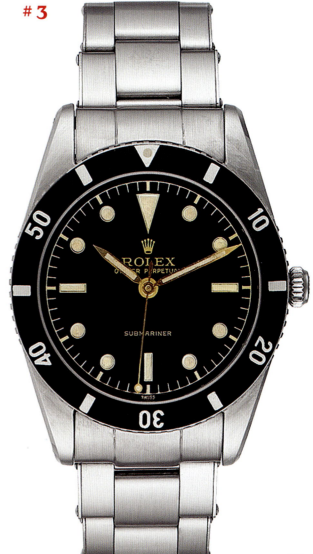

THE BOOK OF ROLEX

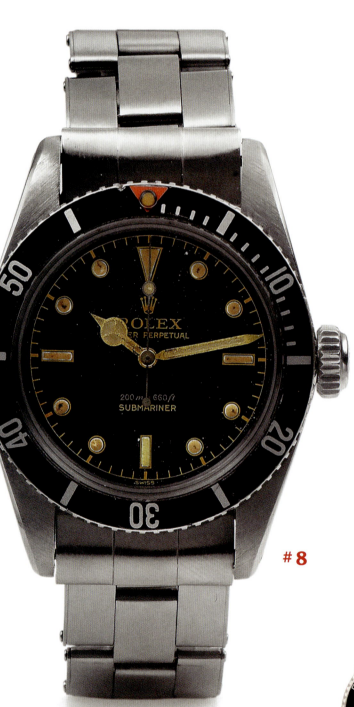

 # 6

 # 7

 # 8

 # 9

 # 10

6 HULK
The version of the SUBMARINER *where both the dial and the bezel are* GREEN.

7 DOUBLE RED
The first SEA-DWELLER *(Ref. 1665), where both* SEA-DWELLER *and* SUBMARINER *are in red on the dial. These watches are very expensive today!*

8 JAMES BOND
In the first Bond movies, 007 *wore the classic and slim version of the new* SUBMARINER *without* CROWN GUARDS.

9 FEET FIRST
A general designation for DIVING WATCHES, *where the maximum depth is applied first in* FEET *then in* METRES.

10 EYE OF THE TIGER
The GMT-MASTER *Ref. 16713 with the* YELLOW AND BRONZE *bezel that looks like the eye of a tiger.*

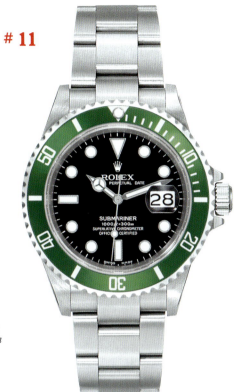

#11 KERMIT
The **50TH**-*anniversary version of the Submariner with the black dial and green bezel is called a* **KERMIT**.

#12 METRES FIRST
A general designation for **DIVING WATCHES**, *where the maximum depth is applied first in* **METRES** *then in* **FEET**.

#13 LEOPARD
A very special **DAYTONA** *with precious stones, and with a* **LEOPARD** *leather strap. This is not a watch for keeping a low profile.*

#14 PANDA
When a **DAYTONA** *has a white dial and black subdials, it's a* **PANDA**.

#15 PATRIZZI
On the Ref. 16520 **DAYTONA** *the subdials can turn a* **CREAMY BROWN**, *as in the watch pictured, which was sold for a record price in 2006 by Italian collector* **OSVALDO PATRIZZI**.

THE BOOK OF
ROLEX

17

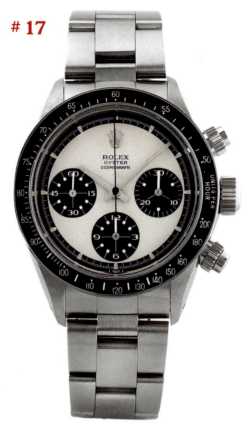

16

18

19

20

16 PRESIDENT
For many years the American presidents would wear the **DAY-DATE II**, *and to this day the model is universally known as* **THE PRESIDENT**.

17 PAUL NEWMAN DIAL
Legend has it that **PAUL NEWMAN** *got a Daytona with this dial from* **HIS WIFE**, *when he took up motor racing late in life, and the model is now known as the* **PAUL NEWMAN DIAL**.

18 PEPSI
When a **GMT-MASTER** *has a bezel in blue and red it's not a Coke but a* **PEPSI**!

19 POLIPETTO
A special version of the Sea-Dweller, also known as **OCTOPUS**, *which Rolex produced for the diving unit of the* **ITALIAN POLICE** *when they celebrated their* **50TH ANNIVERSARY** *in 2008.*

20 PUSSY GALORE
Refers to the **GMT-MASTER**, *when it first came out with the* **BIGGER** *watchcase.*

THE BOOK OF ROLEX

#21

#22

#21 TRIPLE SIX
*Sometimes it's little things that make a Rolex **SOUGHT AFTER**. Like the Sea-Dweller with the reference number **16660**. That's the **DEVIL'S NUMBER** right there.*

#22 SMURF
*Well, what else would you call a **SUBMARINER** with a blue dial and a **BLUE BEZEL**?*

#23 MCQUEEN
***STEVE MCQUEEN** is usually synonymous with the Heuer Monaco he wore in Le Mans, but privately he preferred an **EXPLORER II** with an orange second hour-hand, hence the nickname **MCQUEEN**.*

#24 RAINBOW
*Another special **DAYTONA** fitted with diamonds in the colours of the rainbow. If you like **BLING** in your Rolex, look no further.*

#25 STELLA
*When a **DAY-DATE** has the enamel watchface in powerful colours, it's a **STELLA**.*

#23

#24

#25

THE BOOK OF ROLEX

#26

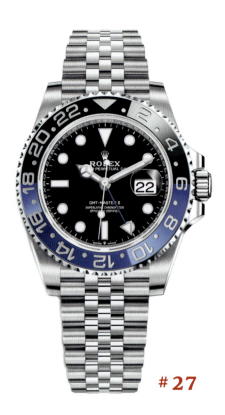

#27

#28

#29

#30

#26 BUBBLE
In 2023, Rolex launched a series of colourful Oyster Perpetual watches. In 2024, all the colours were combined into one model, Ref. 126000, officially named **CELEBRATION DIAL**, *but among Rolex fans, it has become known as the Bubble.*

#27 BATGIRL
A GMT-Master II, Ref. 126710blnr, with a blue and black bezel, black dial, and Jubilee bracelet is called a **BATGIRL** *if it is the model from 2019, which received* **A NEW MOVEMENT**.

#28 POLAR
When an **EXPLORER II** *has a white dial, it is called a* **POLAR**. *Fortunately, it's simple...*

#29 RED SUB
Ref. 1680 was the first Submariner with a date, and if Submariner is **WRITTEN IN RED** *on the dial, it is a* **RED SUB**, *which is among the most sought-after Rolex models among collectors.*

#30 JOHN PLAYER SPECIAL
DAYTONA *in either Ref. 6264 or 6241 in gold with the black exotic dial (the same as on the Paul Newman models) is called a* **JOHN PLAYER SPECIAL**, *named after the cigarette brand that used the* **SAME COLOURS** *on its packaging.*

THE BOOK OF ROLEX

#31

32

#31 EMOJI
The dial is a **PUZZLE***, the date wheel has been replaced by emojis, and the wheel that normally shows the day of the week now has uplifting messages like* **GRATITUDE***,* **FAITH** *and* **LOVE***. Rolex fans are still in* **SHOCK**…

#32 ROOT BEER
When a **GMT-MASTER** *or* **GMT-MASTER II** *has a bezel that is either half brown or half gold, it is called a* **ROOT BEER** *because it resembles the label of the American soft drink of the same name.*

#33 BIG CROWN
Earlier Submariner models had a larger **8-MILLIMETRE CROWN** *on the side and lacked the so-called crown guards.* **SEAN CONNERY** *wore a* **BIG CROWN** *in the Bond film Dr. No.*

#34 FAT LADY
When the GMT-Master II debuted in 1983 as Ref. 16760, it had a case that was **0.5 MILLIMETRES THICKER** *than its predecessor to accommodate the new Calibre 3085 movement, earning it the name* **FAT LADY** *– or* **SOPHIA LOREN***, due to its beautiful curves.*

#35 GREEN LANTERN
In early 2022, Rolex launched their GMT-Master II in a **LEFT-HANDED VERSION** *in green and black. It is also called* **DESTRO***, which means right in Italian, because* **LEFT-HANDED PEOPLE** *wear their watch on their* **RIGHT HAND***.*

145

*Quite possibly the **WEIRDEST** watch Rolex have ever made, as this is a **DAY-DATE** that doesn't display the **DAY** or the **DATE**. Instead, you get **LOVE** and a **HEART**…*

THE BOOK OF
ROLEX

DAY-DATE
PUZZLE-MOTIF

From time to time, Rolex present a new model that breaks with everything we thought we knew about the watchmaker in Geneva, which is the very definition of 'conservative'

'**WHO WOULD WEAR SUCH A WATCH?**' *many might ask. One of them is the American football player* **TOM BRADY**, *who is photographed here with his brand new* **DAY-DATE PUZZLE-MOTIF**.

Your first thought might be 'NO!', but the more you look at it, the more FUN it becomes, and eventually it becomes a CHALLENGE – are you MAN ENOUGH to wear a Puzzle Motif?!?

THE BOOK OF
ROLEX

The only thing Rolex love more than being **CONSERVATIVE** *is being* **UNPREDICTABLE**, *and that is undoubtedly the explanation behind the Puzzle-Motif. No one saw it coming...*

The latest version of Rolex's Day-Date can't actually show the date or the day of the week. In fact, many find it easier to believe it's an extremely well-executed practical joke rather than a genuine creation from Rolex in Geneva, but it is the real deal.

Known as the Day-Date Puzzle-Motif, it comes in three versions: gold, white gold, and Everose. Naturally, it must be mentioned that Rolex could hardly have chosen a more conservative watch upon which to unleash their creative urges. The Day-Date is also known as the Presidents' watch, always made of precious metals, gold or platinum, and has adorned the wrists of world leaders for as long as anyone can remember. For this reason, fans of the traditional model will understandably be horrified by the design of this innovation.

The dial is designed like an unfinished jigsaw puzzle, with coloured sapphires as hour markers, but that's just the beginning, dear reader. It gets much worse! At 12 o'clock, where you would normally see the day of the week (in case you're unsure whether it's Sunday or Tuesday), which the Day-Date can display in no less than 26 languages, you will instead be shown seven uplifting messages: 'Happy', 'Eternity', 'Gratitude', 'Peace', 'Faith', 'Love' and 'Hope'. After some time with the watch, you'll probably remember that 'Gratitude' means Wednesday.

The date is more challenging. Where you would normally find the date on a Day-Date, you will now encounter 31 different emojis, including a four-leaf clover, an eight-ball, a heart, a peace sign, a kissing face, and a Rolex crown. So, the world as you know it no longer exists when you look at your Rolex to see if today is your wedding anniversary and, instead, you're met with a winking and kissing emoji?!?

This is precisely what you might face with the new Day-Date Puzzle-Motif. Upon first seeing it, the initial reaction is disbelief, which turns to slight horror when you realise that it's a genuine Rolex. Then follows mild amazement and, eventually, you can't help but smile. Although we tend to think of Rolex as conservative, they have actually created quite a few models that make you suspect that one or more euphoric substances were part of the design process – such as the Daytona Leopard or the diamond versions of the Yacht-Master. But they pale in comparison to the Puzzle-Motif.

Perhaps it's because no one can be as conservative as Rolex, moving at its own pace, seemingly unaffected by the outside world. Few of us will witness Rolex creating a new model line more than twice in our lifetime, and even then, you'd have to be lucky. Meanwhile, modern frivolities such as smartphones with connectivity are utterly ignored.

Rolex are like the Countess of Grantham in Downton Abbey, conservative but not wanting to be predictable. Maybe that's the explanation behind the Puzzle-Motif – what no one in their wildest dreams had expected from Rolex. And don't think for a moment that the model will be a failure.

Thanks to limited production, prices are already skyrocketing...

> There are still those who find it easier to believe that this must be an elaborate practical joke rather than an actual creation from Rolex in Geneva

*The **DAY-DATE PUZZLE-MOTIF** is also available in **ROSE GOLD**, but only in one size, as the model is only offered in **36 MILLIMETRES**.*

THE CAPTAIN'S WATCH
YACHT-MASTER

If you like swimming in the waves, then you should wear a Submariner, but if you're the captain on the deck, then the Rolex Yacht-Master is for you

When the first **YACHT-MASTER** *was introduced in 1992, it was a sensation. Mostly because it had been* **28 YEARS** *since Rolex had presented a* **BRAND NEW** *model series.*

THE BOOK OF
ROLEX

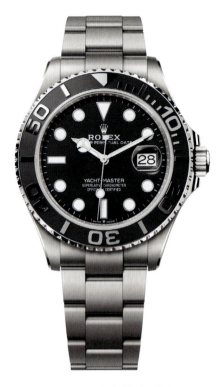

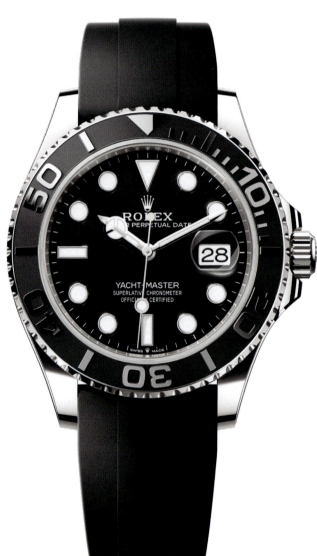

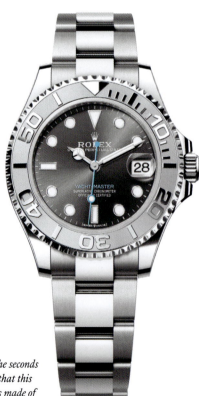

At **FIRST GLANCE**, it looks like brushed **STEEL**, but this version of the Yacht-Master actually has a bracelet and case made of **TITANIUM**.

There have been **SEVERAL** versions of the Yacht-Master with **PRECIOUS STONES**, but now only this one remains in the **YACHT-MASTER** line-up.

Do you see the connection with the **SUBMARINER**? The two share the same movement, so the **YACHT-MASTER** is actually a luxury Submariner.

The **YACHT-MASTER** is available in three sizes: 37, 40 and 42 **MILLIMETRES**, because both men and women can be **CAPTAIN**!

Notice the **BLUE COLOUR** on the seconds hand, which subtly indicates that this version of the Yacht-Master is made of steel and **PLATINUM**.

THE BOOK OF ROLEX

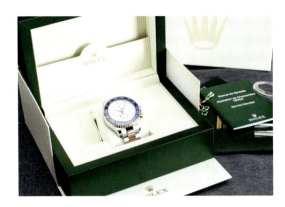

It looks like an older **DAYTONA**, *but it is in fact the first prototype of the* **YACHT-MASTER** *from the 1960s. The size is different too, since the Daytona was 36 millimetres, and the prototype is* **39.5 MILLIMETRES**. *However, Rolex didn't introduce the first* **YACHT-MASTER** *until 1992, based on the* **SUBMARINER**.

When Rolex introduces an entirely new model series, it's a significant event. When the Yacht-Master was introduced in 1992, it had been 28 years since Rolex had presented a new model that wasn't an evolution of an existing one – the Daytona in 1964. From there, it would be another 20 years before the next new model arrived in the form of the Sky-Dweller.

This could easily have been different, as the idea of the Yacht-Master had been simmering for a long time, which resulted in several prototypes in the late '60s. We don't know how many, except that two of them somehow made their way into the public realm, possibly as gifts from Rolex to special business partners. What we do know for certain is that musician and Rolex enthusiast Eric Clapton owned one of them at some point.

There are very few pictures of the Yacht-Master prototype, but in those that exist, we can see that it resembles the Daytona model from that era but with one crucial difference: while the Daytona was 36 millimetres, the prototype for the Yacht-Master was 39.5 millimetres. Rolex abandoned the idea of the Yacht-Master back in the '60s, but it resurfaced in the '80s.

At that time, Rolex were wanting to modernise the Submariner, and the design team ended up with a design very close to what would become the Yacht-Master. Rolex's board was enthusiastic about the design, but when it came down to it, they didn't dare change the Submariner's design – it is the world's most iconic wristwatch.

It was then that someone had a great idea. What if they made a luxury version of the Submariner? The classic Sub was great for use in or under water for the young lads on their jet skis trying to impress girls, while the luxury version was for the captain up on deck. They could call the new model, well, how about the Yacht-Master? That's how it went, and Rolex introduced the new model in the early '90s. The kinship with the Submariner is clear. They both have a 40-millimetre case and use the same Calibre 3135, but the materials are evidently different. While the Submariner can be found in gold, the Yacht-Master is available in platinum, Everose and titanium.

In 2007, Rolex then introduced the Yacht-Master II, which was actually a much bigger news story than the first Yacht-Master. First and foremost, the case is an impressive 44 millimetres, which is due to the movement. It is a chronograph with a built-in programmable timer that counts down from 10 minutes, the typical duration of the start sequence at a regatta. It took Rolex 35,000 working hours (or nearly four years) to develop that function, and with 360 individual parts, it is Rolex's most complicated watch. The timer is operated with the bezel, and if you start the timer too early, you can press the start/stop button at the bottom and then reset, after which the timer in the middle of the dial returns to the nearest minute.

Rolex are, of course, inseparably connected with high-class sailing, and you often see a Yacht-Master or a Yacht-Master II on the wrist of the skipper. But apparently not as often as Rolex wanted, as the model was somewhat surprisingly discontinued in 2024.

> **When the new Yacht-Master was introduced in 1992, it had been 28 years since a new model had been launched, and it would be another 20 years before it happened again**

There was **BLING** *galore in the earlier versions of the* **YACHT-MASTER**, *with a bold contrast to the* **OYSTERFLEX** **BRACELET** *in rubber over a core of* **TITANIUM**, *which was introduced with this very model.*

THE BOOK OF
ROLEX

*If you wanted to buy a new **YACHT-MASTER II**, you're **TOO LATE**. Rolex has decided to **DISCONTINUE** the model in 2024…*

*With a **44-MILLIMETRE** watchcase, the Yacht-Master II is the **BIGGEST** model in the Rolex line-up. A watch that size needs a pretty sturdy wrist, and for many it's just **TOO BIG**.*

*The **PROGRAMMABLE TIMER** in the middle of the dial was created to process the **STARTING SEQUENCE** of a regatta, which typically lasts **10 MINUTES**.*

*The timer that can count down from 10 minutes is seen in the top part of the dial. The **YACHT-MASTER II** requires Rolex's most complicated **MOVEMENT**.*

159

LADY-DATEJUST *is in a category all of its own, like a* FEMININE ANCHOR *in a world where more and more women prefer the traditional and larger* MEN'S MODELS.

THE BOOK OF
ROLEX

FOR THE LADY IN YOUR LIFE
LADY-DATEJUST

Lady-Datejust shows Rolex's feminine side, and is available in a range of sizes, in everything from steel to platinum and with or without precious stones

SOPHIA LOREN *wears her Lady-Datejust in an old Rolex press photo, as she has done for four decades. Like the watch itself she defines* **CLASSIC ELEGANCE**.

THE BOOK OF
ROLEX

The version in **WHITE ROLESOR** *with the* **JUBILEE BRACELET**, *seems both feminine and* **SPORTY** *at the same time.*

EVEROSE GOLD *gives a very special look, whether you choose the version with or without* **GEMSTONES** *around the bezel.*

YES, **OF COURSE**, *you can also get the Lady-Datejust just in* **OYSTERSTEEL**.

More **JEWELLERY THAN A WATCH?** *Here in gold with* **DIAMONDS** *on the mother-of-pearl dial, which is a popular feature on the* **LADY MODELS**.

THE BOOK OF
ROLEX

*As with all models, **MARKETING** is important, and Rolex are the masters of **PROMOTION**. Here are two adverts for the **LADY-DATEJUST**. The one on the right shows its practical application.*

There are those who dismiss the Lady-Datejust as a clever way for Rolex to profit from its brand by making some bling for the wives of the world's wealthy men. Nothing could be further from the truth.

Of course, there is no doubt that the Rolex universe is geared towards men, even though many women wear Rolex, especially vintage versions of popular models like the Daytona with its 36-millimetre case, as well as the Datejust and Submariner. But there is certainly a large audience for what became Rolex's first model dedicated to a female audience.

The first Lady-Datejust was introduced in the late 1950s, and as the name suggests, the design was based on the popular Datejust model from 1945 but adapted for the typically smaller wrists of women. Today, Lady models come in several different sizes. The Lady-Datejust and Lady-Datejust Pearlmaster are available in 26 and 28 millimetres, while the Lady-Datejust also has a 31-millimetre case. Lastly, there is the Lady-Datejust Pearlmaster at 34 millimetres, which is technically a unisex model, although it is undeniably very feminine in gold, white gold, and Everose, adorned with jewels including diamonds.

The Lady-Datejust had the same feature as the Datejust, which was the first watch to display the date in a small window positioned at three o'clock. The first Datejust models, however, took several hours for the date to change, which Rolex solved with the so-called Quickset in 1955, allowing the Lady model to benefit from this feature from the start. It was also a welcome opportunity for Rolex's designers to move in a whole new direction. The colours remain discreet, and the dials are both feminine and elegant in options such as white, pink or black mother-of-pearl. The case itself is milled from a single piece of metal, either 904L steel, gold or Everose – Rolex's patented rose gold, which is a combination of 18-carat gold and steel, as well as, of course, platinum.

No corners were cut with the technical specifications of the Lady-Datejust model. It is powered by the Calibre 2235 which is Rolex's most compact movement, primarily so that it could fit into the 26 millimetre case (although it now only comes in one size, namely 28 millimetres). Nonetheless, it has a 48-hour power reserve, which is quite impressive given the size. And when Rolex say that all their watches are COSC-tested, that naturally includes the Lady-Datejust. This means that every single example has undergone 15 days of rigorous testing at the Contrôle Officiel Suisse des Chronomètres, an independent non-profit organisation that tests the precision of all watch movements and models. In fact, only three per cent of Swiss watches undergo this test, but all of Rolex's do. It is hard to imagine anyone diving with the watch, but if it should happen, it is actually water-resistant down to 100 metres, which is 40 metres more than the maximum depth that can be reached with modern diving equipment. In other words, it is a genuine Rolex through and through.

In 1992, Rolex launched the more exclusive Lady-Datejust Pearlmaster, which is always adorned with diamonds or other gemstones. For those who want a Rolex that is also a piece of jewellery, the Lady-Datejust is perfect.

> **Every single Lady-Datejust is certified by the COSC, and is waterproof to 100 metres' depth, 40 metres more than is possible with modern diving equipment**

THE BOOK OF
ROLEX

*This model is in **WHITE GOLD**, used for the **CASE**, **BEZEL** and the central section of the **BRACELET**, with diamonds on the bezel – very **STYLISH**.*

'DIAMONDS ARE A GIRL'S BEST FRIEND', *as Marilyn Monroe sang, and here we might have reached the **LIMIT** of how many a wristwatch **CAN HOLD**!*

PREVIOUSLY, *the Lady-Datejust was available in **26**, **28** AND **31 MILLIMETRES**. Now it is only available in **28 MILLIMETRES**, but the regular Datejust is available in **31 MILLIMETRES**.*

THE BOOK OF
ROLEX

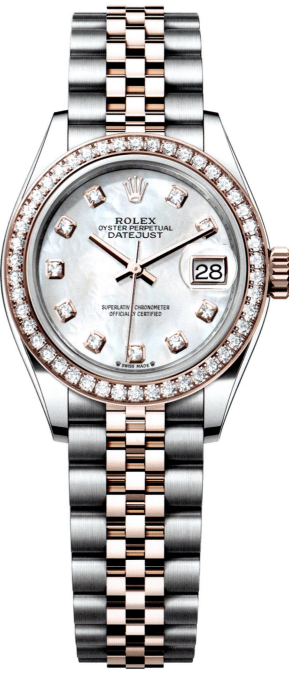

The Lady-Datejust is also available with the exclusive **JUBILEE BRACELET**, *which is almost a piece of* **JEWELLERY** *in itself.*

LADY-DATEJUST *is a genuine Rolex, and as such it is of course certified by the* **COSC**, *where every single watch is tested rigorously for 15 days before being* **APPROVED**.

SEA-DWELLER *works best on a big wrist, but then you get a* **DIVING WATCH** *that can travel with you down to a depth of* **1,220 METRES** *or* **4,000 FEET**, *and takes well over a year to produce from* **START TO FINISH.**

THE BOOK OF
ROLEX

SUBMARINER ULTRA
SEA-DWELLER

Sea-Dweller sits above the Submariner, meant to fit on the wrist of the professional diver as Rolex's most authentic 'tool watch' capable of diving to 1,220 metres

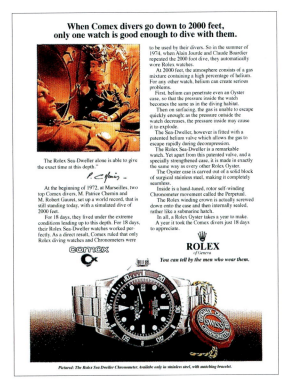

Rolex announcing the **WORLD RECORD** *set by the Comex divers, who spent* **18 DAYS** *in conditions similar to a depth of 2,000 feet. The enormous pressure would crush any watch, but not a* **SEA-DWELLER**, *thanks to the innovative* **HELIUM ESCAPE VALVE**.

THE BOOK OF
ROLEX

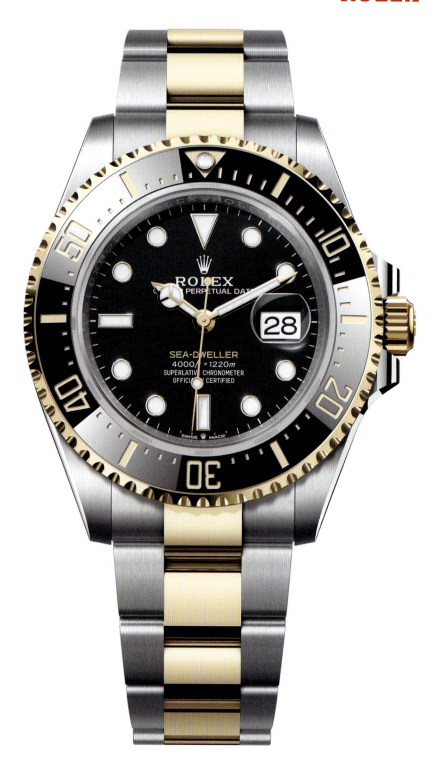

FOR MANY YEARS, the Sea-Dweller was only available in **STEEL**, but that has changed, and now there is a version in both gold **AND STEEL**. Rolex have also managed to create a **CYCLOPS LENS** that can withstand the pressure at a depth of **1,220 METRES**.

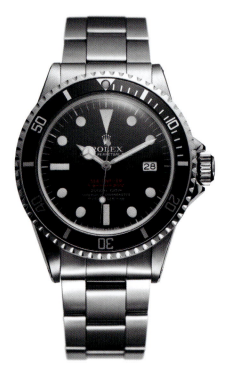

The first generation of the **SEA-DWELLER** *was certified for* **2,000 FEET**, *or* **610 METRES**, *of depth, which was a record at the time.*

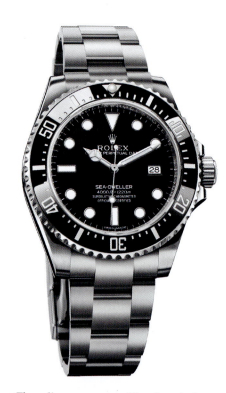

The earlier **SEA-DWELLER** *did not have the date under the so-called* **CYCLOPS LENS** *because it could not withstand the* **ENORMOUS PRESSURE**.

THE BOOK OF ROLEX

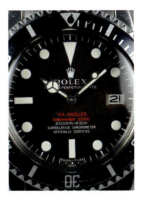

The first Sea-Dweller is known as a **DOUBLE RED** *when the name is written in two lines in red. The* **CYCLOPS LENS** *didn't appear before the 2017 edition. In the middle, there's the so-called* **HELIUM ESCAPE VALVE**, *developed specifically for the Sea-Dweller to handle the pressure at* **GREAT DEPTHS**.

In the 1960s, professional divers began to request a wristwatch that could withstand the enormous pressure at depths of 300 metres. Rolex already had the Submariner, but even that was not sufficient. It was clear that something new was needed. The solution came in the form of the Sea-Dweller, which exists in several different models. The first was the Sea-Dweller 2000 – or Rolex Oyster Perpetual Sea-Dweller Submariner 2000, to give it its full name.

This model is known among enthusiasts as the 'Double Red' due to the two lines of red text on the dial, and was rated for 2,000 feet, or 610 metres. In the late 1970s, it was followed by the Sea-Dweller 4000, which could handle 4,000 feet or 1,220 metres. This model has been part of the standard equipment for divers from the legendary COMEX – Compagnie Maritime d'Expertises, founded in 1961 by deep-sea diver Henri-Germain Delauze. The name Sea-Dweller is actually a term used for deep-sea divers who can spend several weeks below the ocean's surface, as is often the case with COMEX divers, for example, during the construction of oil platforms. The depth record is still held by COMEX diver Theo Mavrostomos, who reached a depth of 701 metres. The record attempt was carried out in a pressure chamber on land, but it still took 43 days and allowed the study of the extreme stresses caused by the enormous pressure, such as on the central nervous system. It goes without saying that Mavrostomos wore a Rolex Sea-Dweller 4000, which functioned flawlessly throughout the experiment.

As the name suggests, the Sea-Dweller was developed based on the Submariner but is capable of withstanding even higher pressure. Part of the explanation lies in a special feature known as the helium escape valve – a feature not always present in the first models from the late '60s. Its successor, the 1978 Sea-Dweller 4000, always has the helium escape valve, proving that it is possible to find a simple solution to an unusual problem. Deep-sea divers breathe a gas mixture containing helium so that their lungs can handle the enormous pressure. The problem with helium is that it finds its way through even the tightest seals, eventually ending up inside even the best diving watch. This is not an issue as long as the watch remains at the ocean floor, but during ascent the helium gas expands and can easily destroy a movement. Many solutions to this problem have been developed over the years – some divers' watches have an extra crown that can be unscrewed to release the helium gas. However, not all divers remember to do this.

Typically for Rolex, they found a simple solution in the form of a spring-loaded valve. This allows the microscopic helium particles to escape and is a mechanical solution that works automatically, regardless of the fact that only COMEX divers really need it. Nevertheless, a mechanical watch is all about fascination.

This does not change the fact that a Rolex Sea-Dweller is a technical triumph and an important part of modern diving history. It is also a pure 'tool watch', and for many years it was only available in steel, whereas today there is also a version in gold. But no diamonds! That's the limit!

> Sea-Dweller is an important part of diving history and a pure 'tool watch', which for many years was only available in steel, although it is now also available in gold

Rolex produced five **PROTOTYPES** *of the Deepsea Challenge for* **JAMES CAMERON'S** *expedition. Note the writing on the dial – it will go to 39,370 feet, or* **12,000 METRES'** *depth.*

THE BOOK OF
ROLEX

THE KING OF DIVING WATCHES
DEEPSEA

When the Hollywood director and explorer James Cameron took a prototype Deepsea Challenge to the deepest point in the ocean, he created a Rolex legend

It's easy to see why the first **DEEPSEA** *remained a prototype, because it's pretty difficult* **TO TELL THE TIME** *due to the thick glass. However, it did set a record which was to stand for* **HALF A CENTURY**.

THE BOOK OF ROLEX

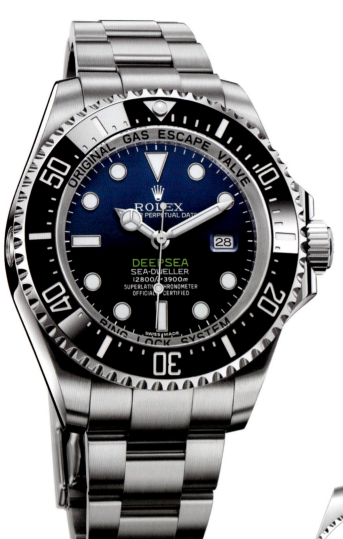

NO, *you're not drunk – this is what it looks like when you try to tell the time on the original* **ROLEX DEEPSEA SPECIAL.**

The Deepsea is also available in an **18-CT GOLD VERSION**, *with a bezel and dial in blue Cerachrom, featuring a special* **SATIN-LIKE FINISH.**

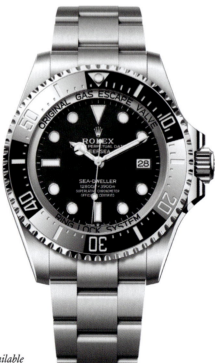

The **D-BLUE EDITION** *from 2014 is the civilian version of the watch that accompanied* **JAMES CAMERON** *to the bottom of* **CHALLENGER DEEP**. *It features a special dial that transitions from* **BLUE TO BLACK**, *mimicking the experience of diving into the depths.*

REST ASSURED, *the Sea-Dweller is still available in* **BLACK AND STEEL**, *without gold or frills, for those who need the ultimate diving watch, rated for depths up to* **3,900 METRES**.

The **ENGINEERING** *is crazy! Note the thickness of the* **SAPPHIRE CRYSTAL** *glass, necessary to withstand the enormous pressure at* **FOUR KILOMETRES'** *depth.*

THE BOOK OF
ROLEX

The original **ROLEX DEEPSEA SPECIAL** *that reached the* **CHALLENGER DEEP** *in 1960 with* **JACQUES PICCARD**. *The strange bubble-shaped glass was necessary to withstand the enormous pressure. The watch was attached to the outside of Piccard's submarine, the* **TRIESTE**, *and worked perfectly throughout the entire trip.*

How could Rolex possibly turn away James Cameron, when he asked them to create a watch that would go to the Challenger Deep, the deepest point in the Mariana Trench? Cameron is not just the director of Hollywood blockbusters like *Avatar* and *Titanic*. He's also a passionate diver and explorer.

Cameron's submarine had been christened *Deepsea Challenger*, and during the entire trip he wore a new experimental diving watch around his wrist. However, this wasn't the only Rolex that went along for the ride. Outside the protective hull of the submarine, a robot arm held a watch just like the one on Cameron's wrist. Rolex had named the model the Deepsea Challenge. The Mariana Trench is an enormous ravine around the Mariana Islands. The Challenger Deep sits at a depth of 11,000 metres, which is hard to comprehend. But if you placed the world's highest mountain, Mount Everest, on the bottom of the Challenger Deep, there would still be two kilometres from the top of the mountain to the surface of the ocean.

It's not the first time Rolex have taken on the mighty depths of the Mariana Trench. French explorer Jacques Piccard became the first to reach the Challenger Deep on 23 January 1960, aboard the bathyscaphe *Trieste*. The depth of 10,916 metres set a new diving world record, and on the outside of the hull, the *Trieste* carried an experimental model of the new Rolex Oyster, named the Deepsea Special. When the watch was once again returned to the surface, it was still working perfectly, which was an achievement that was to stand for more than half a century.

When creating the prototype watch for James Cameron, Rolex used the current Deepsea as a starting point, and then started calculating how to make it strong enough to resist the enormous pressure. When approaching 15,000 metres, gigantic forces are released. The pressure on the crystals in the movement is an unbelievable 17 tons, and the back of the watchcase has to withstand 23 tons of pressure – or the equivalent of 14 family cars, stacked on top of each other.

One of Rolex's designers was instructed to focus on the dimensions of the prototype, which apparently led to some heated discussions with the engineers. It was obvious form the beginning that the Deepsea Challenge would need some generous dimensions. The enormous pressure also presented some unique challenges when engineering the rotating bezel into the construction. The crown also had to be redesigned, since the normal crown would seem much too small. And because of the pressure, the Rolex logo could not be stamped into the crown, as is usually the case. Instead it was laser-engraved, so as not to weaken the steel.

Rolex watchmakers usually have plenty of time when designing a new watch, but this time they had just four weeks. All in all, five prototypes were built and tested at 1,500 bars, the pressure at 15,000 metres' depth, to give a healthy safety margin. There must have been some tense moments before Cameron returned to the surface.

Rolex engineers concluded that the prototypes still worked perfectly, both those that had been inside and outside *Deepsea Challenger*. Based on this technical triumph, the engineers then started work on what would become the Rolex Sea-Dweller Deepsea – the king of diving watches.

> **If you placed Mount Everest at the bottom of the Challenger Deep, there would still be two kilometres from the top of the mountain to the surface of the ocean**

JAMES CAMERON *returned to the surface after his journey to the bottom of* **CHALLENGER DEEP.** *Naturally, on his wrist was a* **ROLEX DEEPSEA.**

Normally, only your watchmaker can see the MOVEMENT in your Rolex, but the PERPETUAL 1908 is equipped with a TRANSPARENT CASEBACK, allowing you to appreciate the fine mechanics.

ROLEX'S DRESS WATCH
PERPETUAL 1908

It's not every day that Rolex introduces a new model series, but the Perpetual 1908 marks the beginning of an entirely new family of 'dress watches'

WHICH ROLEX *do you choose if you're not interested in diving or mountaineering? The* **PERPETUAL 1908** *is a dress watch for those who prefer* **OPERA** *and similar pursuits.*

THE BOOK OF
ROLEX

The classic look in **BLACK AND GOLD.** *The size is* **39 MILLIMETRES,** *just below the traditional size for* **SPORTS WATCHES.**

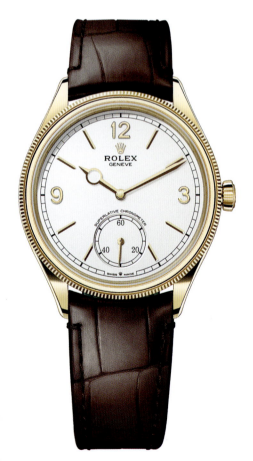

In **WHITE GOLD,** *it is almost* **DISCREET;** *however, the choice of bracelet is* **SIMPLE,** *as the Perpetual 1908 is only available with an* **ALLIGATOR-LEATHER STRAP.**

ONLY THE BEST *is good enough, so the top model of Perpetual 1908 is, of course, in* **PLATINUM.** *The disc itself is described as guilloché, which gives a special* **THREE-DIMENSIONAL EFFECT.**

Notice the black dial, which has a special **MATT FINISH.** *The watch strap features the so-called* **DUALCLASP,** *ensuring that your watch always sits* **CORRECTLY ON YOUR WRIST.**

THE BOOK OF ROLEX

The brand new **CALIBRE 7140** *powers the Perpetual 1908 and has everything you expect in a Rolex. It offers a* **66**-**HOUR** *power reserve, and the so-called* **PERPETUAL ROTOR** *is made of* **GOLD**.

'Perpetual' is a nod back to the first models that had a perpetual rotor, while 1908 was the year the founder Hans Wilsdorf came up with the name Rolex. The new model series was presented in 2023, and at the same time, the previous series of dress watches – Cellini, a series that few even knew existed – was discontinued.

Perhaps this is because the Cellini models were never really associated with anything specific and thus did not develop their own story, whereas the Daytona is linked with motorsport and Paul Newman, the Air-King with the 'Great Escape', and the Deepsea with James Cameron. The most dramatic event a Cellini owner probably ever experienced was arriving late for an opera performance, which doesn't quite compare to diving 12,800 metres to the Challenger Deep.

In many ways, the new Perpetual series resembles the Cellini, although the Cellini always seemed like a separate watch brand and for some reason was never mentioned when Rolex presented its line-up. With the Perpetual 1908, it seems Rolex have finally made the series part of the family, creating a series of watches that simply exude elegance.

It therefore follows that it also provides everything you expect from a Rolex. So, it is water-resistant to 50 metres, COSC-certified and, additionally, it is a Superlative Chronometer, which is Rolex's own certification, conducted to stricter standards than COSC.

Then there is, of course, the design, which is a classic dress watch with Arabic numerals at 12, 3 and 9, and a small seconds hand placed in a subdial at 6 o'clock. The fluted bezel on the front matches the one on the back (which is glass), allowing a view of the new movement – Calibre 7140 – and the enjoyment of Rolex's perpetual rotor, in gold or white gold, depending on the model.

Another interesting detail is in the version with the black dial, which has a special matt finish – a detail that one might overlook at first glance. It resembles the look of older vintage models that have faded after many years of use. And then, of course, there is the alligator-leather strap, which, regardless of colour, has a green interior in coloured calfskin – again, a detail only the wearer will know about. It is naturally equipped with the Rolex Dualclasp, ensuring a better fit on the wrist.

According to Rolex, the Perpetual 1908 models that have been launched are just the beginning, so it is likely that the line-up will be expanded in the coming years. For many, the new series may seem out of place in the line-up dominated by sports watches like the Daytona, but consider the design of the first Oyster Perpetual and Explorer models, and it becomes suddenly clear where the inspiration for the design came from.

For those who appreciate the older models and their simple design without frills or numerous functions that few of us actually use, the Perpetual 1908 is the answer. Simple, elegant and exclusive – especially in platinum – just as a Rolex should be, and at 39 millimetres, it is large enough to be modern but not so large as to be ostentatious. In reality, the Perpetual 1908 is just Rolex doing what Rolex have always done.

> **The problem with dress watches is that they don't have a history. The most dramatic thing the owner of a dress watch has probably done is arrive late at the opera**

The dial on the **PLATINUM MODEL** *has a special finish created with a technique Rolex calls* **GUILLOCHAGE***, which reflects light in a unique way.*

CELLINI *is one of the top models with* **MOON PHASE** *on the* **DIAL**, *and the moon itself on the moon phase is naturally made from a real* **METEORITE**!

THE BOOK OF ROLEX

ROLEX'S SECRET MODEL
CELLINI

The Cellini models were the classic dress watch, but also a watch for a small group of connoisseurs, that even Rolex would often forget about...

The other model in the **CELLINI SERIES** *was the classic* **ROLEX PRINCE**, *also known as the* '**DOCTOR'S WATCH**' *due to its separate seconds hand. The Prince is one of Rolex's oldest models and an important part of the brand's success.*

THE BOOK OF
ROLEX

The **CELLINI MOONPHASE** *featured a complication, which was unusual in itself, as Rolex* **VERY RARELY** *include such features.*

BLACK ON BLACK! *Once again, the Cellini Time model has a special depth due to its* **DESIGN**, *where the seconds are marked inside* **THE DIAL** *rather than on the* **OUTER EDGE.**

The fluted bezel along **THE EDGE** *of the dial is one of many classic details on a* **CELLINI**, *just like the crown without* **CROWN GUARDS.**

EVEROSE GOLD *and an alligator-leather strap – nothing could be more* **ELEGANT.** *The Cellini Time displays the time and* **NOTHING ELSE.**

The **CELLINI DUAL-TIME** *not only displays the date but also features a small* **SUN AND MOON** *indicator to show whether it is* **DAY OR NIGHT** *in the time zone you left.*

THE BOOK OF
ROLEX

The **MOONPHASE** *was the big news from Rolex in the* **CELLINI SERIES IN 2017,** *as it featured a* **COMPLICATION** *that shows you the phases of the Moon. The moon itself is made from a* **METEORITE** *that is several hundred million years old, and impossible to replicate on* **EARTH.**

For most of us, the Rolex brand is inextricably linked with sports watches like the Submariner and dress watches based on sports models like the Datejust and Day-Date. However, Rolex had a secret in the form of the Cellini series, which were uncompromising dress watches that demanded a bespoke suit. The first Cellini models were introduced back in 1975, and the name came from the Italian Renaissance artist Benvenuto Cellini, who was, among many other things, a goldsmith, a composer and a sculptor.

It was notoriously difficult to get an overview of the different Cellini models, because they moved in all directions and, unusually for Rolex, seemed to be driven by fashion. Over the years, Cellini models have been introduced for both men and women, but Rolex were always very sparing with information about them. In the traditional historical overview from Rolex, not a single word was mentioned about Cellini. Nevertheless, the series was re-introduced in 2014 at Baselworld. There were three models, called Time, Date and Dual Time. The last one features two time zones and an indicator for whether it is day or night in the time zone you have just left.

While almost all other Rolex models are delivered with a bracelet, the Cellini always had an alligator-leather strap, just like the new Perpetual 1908 series. And while the typical Rolex is very masculine and functional, a Cellini is nothing but elegant. One of the few places where the Cellini models have something in common with the rest of the Rolex family is the movement, which borrowed quite a bit from Rolex's Calibre 3135. In other words, it is an automatic movement with the blue Parachrom hairspring, just like in many of Rolex's sports models.

Like all other models from Rolex, the Cellini models are waterproof, but only to 50 metres, which probably doesn't matter much – after all, few people would wear a watch with a leather strap while swimming in the Mediterranean unless it happens by accident.

It was undoubtedly a model that divided Rolex enthusiasts, and it would not be wrong to say that it is very much a watch for connoisseurs. The Cellini was about classic elegance and was the watch you could wear to formal events that require a tuxedo or suit, as a sort of finishing touch for the well-dressed gentleman.

A Cellini is always made of precious metal, in this case either white gold or Rolex's special rose gold, called Everose gold. The classic lines are evident everywhere, and yet there are details that made the last generation of Cellini something special – like the way the seconds are not marked on the edge of the dial, but on a smaller circle inside the watch, giving the dial a particular depth.

Displaying the date like the other Rolex models is also not something Cellini does. In fact, it is only the Cellini Date that shows the date in the classic way, with a subdial, as was done before Rolex's own Datejust was introduced and set a new standard for such features, which has been widely imitated since.

The Cellini is the watch that the true Rolex enthusiast has in their collection but probably wears very rarely, and it would not be an understatement to call it Rolex's secret model. You had to know it existed to be able to order one.

Now the Cellini series has been discontinued and replaced by the Perpetual 1908, which can be found on Rolex's website. That honour never befell the Cellini models, without anyone being entirely sure why.

> Rolex was extremely sparing with information about Cellini. In the historical overview of Rolex's models, not a single word is mentioned about Cellini

THE BOOK OF
ROLEX

*The **PRINCE SERIES** was originally introduced in 1928, but disappeared in the early 1940s. In 2005 Rolex **REINTRODUCED** the model, but it's still one of the most elusive models.*

THE DOCTOR'S WATCH

It was one of the founding models from Rolex, and now the doctor's watch is back

Today, Rolex are inextricably linked with concepts like the Submariner and the Daytona, but it all began with the Prince series, which few have heard of. It would not be incorrect to say that the Prince model laid the foundation for Rolex's success long before terms like 'Oyster' and 'Perpetual' came into play. The Prince is recognisable by its rectangular case, with the time displayed in the upper part and the seconds in the lower part. This feature earned it the nickname 'doctor's watch', as the separate seconds hand was extremely useful for doctors when measuring patients' pulses. It was also the first watch to receive the coveted Chronometer certification, which was a deliberate part of Rolex founder Hans Wilsdorf's strategy to deliver the highest quality.

The first Prince model was introduced in 1928 with a manual movement, which was shortly after replaced by an automatic movement. Rolex continuously introduced new models in the series, but it was certainly not a watch for the average person. For the price of a Rolex Prince, it was actually possible to buy a small car!

In the following years, Rolex experienced rapid development with milestones such as the first Oyster models, and by the late 1940s, the Prince model quietly disappeared from the line-up. However, in 2005, it made a comeback as part of the Cellini series. Did we say that Rolex do not give in to fashion trends, such as making a transparent caseback to view the movement? That is also true, except for the Prince model, which gives it that extra something that none of the others have.

The Prince was available in gold, white gold, or Everose Gold, although very few of Rolex's dealers had a piece in stock. The Prince series was discontinued along with the Cellini, but who knows if it will one day return as part of the Perpetual 1908?

*The **PRINCE** is the only Rolex where you can actually admire the **MOVEMENT** through the glass on the back of the watchcase.*

TUDOR HERITAGE CHRONOGRAPH *is designed along the lines of the brand's best-known model,* **MONTE CARLO**, *which is sought after by collectors.*

ROLEX'S FORGOTTEN BROTHER
TUDOR

Tudor is often overlooked, but it is a Rolex in a bolder package, manufactured in the same place as its exclusive big brother, and it has its own unique style

The **HERITAGE ADVISOR** *is a re-issue of the original Advisor from 1957, but now in 42 millimetre. The small* **INDICATOR** *at 3 o'clock displays the power reserve for the* **BUILT-IN ALARM.**

On the left, an older **PELAGOS**, Tudor's version of the **SUBMARINER**. Note that it still has the 'screw-down crown' like the first **SUBMARINERS**.

HERITAGE CHRONO BLUE *is another model from* **TUDOR**, *which will probably become a* **SOUGHT-AFTER** *classic before long.*

MONTE CARLO *is Tudor's most sought-after classic model, and vintage ones are traded at quite* **REASONABLE PRICES**.

THE BOOK OF
ROLEX

On the right, the very first **TUDOR WATCH**, *the Oyster Prince, known as* **THE DOCTOR'S WATCH**. *In the middle, Rolex founder,* **HANS WILSDORF**, *announces the introduction of* **TUDOR**. *The movements used to be from ETA, but these days Tudor produce their* **OWN CALIBRE**.

There is a hint of Rolex in Tudor, but at the same time, the brand has its own style. At Rolex, it would be considered a great compliment to be called conservative, and here the development progresses very deliberately and slowly. Tudor is different. The brand was created by Hans Wilsdorf, the founder of Rolex, with the idea of producing a watch with a quality that could match Rolex's, but at a lower price. This is still the case, but Tudor also do things that Rolex would never dream of, such as re-issuing classic models. This has led to the revival of Tudor, which had almost been forgotten.

A Rolex is expensive because customers are willing to pay for the assurance that comes with choosing a brand that guarantees your children can get parts for the watch many years after you have passed away. Previously, Tudor used older movements from Rolex and was produced at Rolex, but now they have developed their own movements and produce their watches independently.

Seventy years after Wilsdorf had the idea, Tudor thrive securely under Rolex's wing. Rolex and Tudor are manufactured and sold side by side, and it is not difficult to find elements from older Rolex models that Tudor uses in a new way, such as the bezel from the Daytona. But from there, the two are like night and day. Rolex stands for safety, predictability and steady evolution, where nothing unexpected happens, and everything is considered down to the smallest detail, without ever compromising on materials. That is why a Rolex holds its value so well. It is also why it is so expensive.

Tudor are more expressive, more experimental, and readily launch radical designs that follow trends and fashion. They often blend historical design elements in a new way, such as the black dial with red graphics on the Fastrider – which is also available in red with army green – within the bezel borrowed from Rolex's Daytona.

The first Oyster model came out in 1947. The brand 'The Tudor' was actually registered in 1926 by a jeweller in Switzerland at the behest of Hans Wilsdorf, who officially bought the rights to the name ten years later. Since Tudor was intended as a more affordable Rolex, they used movements from the small Swiss specialist ETA, but today they manufacture their own calibres. Tudor's Calibre MT5621, with a power reserve of 70 hours, shows the development the brand has undergone since 2010 when they began reinterpreting classic models from the '50s, '60s and '70s. This includes the Heritage Advisor with the built-in alarm from 1957, which was originally 35 millimetres but is now available in a more modern 42 millimetres. And of course, Tudor still have their classic version of Rolex's timeless Submariner, here called the Pelagos. The new movement is the first to be developed in-house by Tudor and was presented in the North Flag model, which has a glass back so you can see the movement at work. All in all, it makes good sense to have two watch brands that are different and therefore attract two different customer groups, not least because Tudor can borrow a little from Rolex from time to time – also because the demand for Rolex has grown to a size where they have difficulty supplying watches to customers.

> **Unlike Rolex, Tudor are more expressive and more radical in their design, which follows trends and fashion, blending colours and textures in new ways**

THE BOOK OF
ROLEX

BLACK BAY GMT *is Tudor's answer to the* **GMT-MASTER**, *and it even comes in a 'Pepsi' version, allowing you to keep track of multiple* **TIME ZONES**.

BLACK BAY, *seen here in the so-called* **PINK VERSION**, *is Tudor's answer to the* **DAYTONA**. *Tudor often borrow* **DIALS AND MOVEMENTS** *from older Rolex models.*

Of course, you can get both **BLING AND MOTHER-OF-PEARL** *with Tudor. You just need to choose the model they call* **ROYAL**.

RANGER *is the equivalent of Rolex's* **OYSTER PERPETUAL** *models – an elegant and solid watch, without superfluous* **FRILLS**.

TUDOR *naturally also have a version of Rolex's classic Submariner, called* **PELAGOS**, *but the movement comes from an older* **SUBMARINER**.

*If a **ROLEX** is too conservative, then a **TUDOR** may be the solution.* **THE QUALITY** *is the same as a Rolex, and Tudors are produced at the Rolex factories in* **SWITZERLAND**.

ANDREW BASTAWROUS *received the Rolex Laureate in 2016 for his work with* PEEK VISION, *which helps diagnose eye diseases in impoverished areas of* AFRICA.

THE SELFLESS
BENEFACTOR

Rolex are not just about expensive watches; every year, they donate millions to support artists and people around the world who are making a difference

Ever since Mercedes Gleitze swam across the English Channel with a Rolex on her wrist in 1927, Rolex have spent considerable amounts supporting the arts and people passionate about making a difference around the world. Only a small handful of people know how much Rolex invest in this way each year, as the company is extremely secretive when it comes to specifying amounts for the many activities it funds. Since Rolex are owned by a foundation, they do not have to disclose how much they earn or how much they spend on charitable efforts. The foundation is considered to be among the world's ten largest philanthropists, and there are two main models for distributing funds.

One is the Rolex Awards for Enterprise. Since 1976, this programme has supported 130 entrepreneurs across a wide range of fields. The project was created to celebrate the 50th anniversary of the waterproof Rolex Oyster watch. The common theme is that projects benefit, for example, local communities, and there are no strict limits on what can be supported. This could include the establishment of small businesses that generate jobs and income for many, or classic funding in the form of money for research across diverse topics such as health, the environment, and cultural history. In 2009, the programme was expanded with additional funding under the name Young Laureates, supporting young people aged 18 to 30 who have ideas for tackling global challenges. Grants are typically awarded in portions of 100,000 Swiss francs (approx. £90,000) and 50,000 Swiss francs (approx. £45,000). In 2016, a total of 2,322 projects from

144 countries applied for support, and ten made it through the selection process. One example of a project funded by Rolex is a system for diagnosing eye diseases using a mobile phone. Peek Vision, founded by Andrew Bastawrous, received funding and support in 2016 to train local teachers to use the system to benefit the poor in southern Africa.

The second model is the Rolex Mentor and Protégé Arts Initiative. This programme aims to connect established artists from seven art disciplines with young talents in a mentor–mentee relationship, benefiting both parties. Founded in 2002, the long-term goal of this philanthropic work is to support global cultural development. Selected established artists choose, in collaboration with Rolex, which young artist will have the chance to learn from the master, rather than talented youngsters applying to be taken under the wing of an established artist. At a minimum, the two spend six weeks together within a calendar year, but in practice, the programme often fosters friendships between artists, and for many, the contact and recognition from Rolex serve as the launching point for an international career.

Another important part of Rolex's charitable efforts, which is not mentioned anywhere on Rolex's official website or in the company's press releases, is their support for various orphanages. We may never know the extent of this support, but Rolex's founder, Hans Wilsdorf, grew up as an orphan. The foundation he created still owns Rolex, and since he bequeathed his shares to the foundation before his death, Rolex today has no shareholders.

> Peek Vision is an example of a project that has received funding from Rolex. It is a system for diagnosing eye diseases using a mobile phone

Copyright © 2025 ACC Art Books
World copyright reserved

ISBN: 978 1 78884 310 2

First published in the Danish language under the title *Den store bog om ROLEX* in 2024 by People's Press, Copenhagen
© 2024 Jens Høy and Christian Frost; © 2024 People's Press, Copenhagen

This English translation published by ACC Art Books Ltd in 2025 by agreement with the Kontext Agency

The rights of Jens Høy and Christian Frost to be identified as authors of this work have been asserted by them in accordance with the Copyright, Designs and Patents Act 1988

All rights reserved. No part of this publication may be reproduced, stored in a retrieval system, or transmitted in any form or by any means electronic, mechanical, photocopying, recording or otherwise, without the prior permission of the publisher.

Neither the authors nor the publisher of this book are affiliated with Rolex SA or Montres Tudor SA. Rolex SA and Montres Tudor SA are in no way responsible for the content or the indicated prices that appear in the book. The completed book has not been submitted to Rolex SA or Montres Tudor SA.

The authors and publisher gratefully acknowledge the permission granted to reproduce the copyright material in this book. Every effort has been made to trace copyright holders and to obtain their permission for the use of copyright material. The publisher apologises for any errors or omissions in the text and would be grateful if notified of any corrections that should be incorporated in future reprints or editions of this book.

A CIP catalogue record for this book is available from the British Library

All the photos in this book are promotional and press images from Rolex with the exception of the pictures on pages: 30–32 (© Phillips Auctioneers LLC); 46, 48–52, 118–27, 170 (Mads Dreier); 96, 98–99, 168 (Jens Høy); 147 (Getty Images)

English edition
Editor: Sue Bennett
Production: Steve Farrow
Translator: Christian Frost

EU GPSR Authorised Representative:
Easy Access System Europe Oü, 16879218
Address: Mustamäe tee 50, 10621 Tallinn, Estonia
Email: gpsr@easproject.com Tel: +358 40 500 3575

Printed in China by Toppan Leefung Printing Ltd
for ACC Art Books Ltd, Woodbridge, Suffolk, UK
www.accartbooks.com

Jens Høy is a Rolex connoisseur – a fashion and lifestyle journalist known for his work with the Danish newspaper *Berlingske* and its business magazine, *Erhversbladet*, among many others. Christian Frost is a journalist and author, renowned for his Erik Otto Falster crime series, especially *God Is Just Dog Spelled Backwards* and *The Arab Who Was White as Snow*.

Together they present *The Book of Rolex*, which is for collectors and enthusiasts, as well as an introduction to the timeless brand.